DONE DEAL

DISCIPLE'S

JOURNAL

ON A

CHRISTIAN'S

IDENTITY IN

CHRIST

JEFF KINLEY

David C. Cook Publishing Co.
Colorado Springs, CO/Paris, Ontario

GREAT GROUPS
The Main Thing Series
Done Deal Journal
© 1995 David C. Cook Publishing Co. All rights reserved.

Published by David C. Cook Church Ministry Resources,
a division of Cook Communications Ministries International.
Colorado Springs, CO 80918
Cable address: DCCOOK
Edited by Randy Southern
Cover and interior design: Jeff Sharpton, PAZ Design Group
Cover illustration: Ken Cuffe
Interior illustration: Paula Becker
Printed in U.S.A.

ISBN: 0-7814-5198-1

TABLE OF Contents

ACKNOWLEDGMENTS

A special thanks to Chris, Eric, Melinda, and Anita
—my "prayer team"—
who faithfully encouraged and prayed for me
throughout the writing of this book.
I am deeply grateful for your labor of love.

DEDICATION

To Beverly,

my precious bride
God's perfect gift to me
who faithfully reminds me
who I really am in Christ.
I love you.

INTRODUCTION

Dear Friend,

Allow me to do you a big favor and introduce you to yourself. That's right, yourself. No, not the you others say you are or even who you may think you are, but the real you. The you God says you are. The new you in Christ. Through the pages of this book and your own Bible, you will experience a face-to-face encounter with the person God made you to be through His Son Jesus. Over the next several weeks, you will discover things about your relationship with God that you never dreamed were true.

Unfortunately, today many Christian young people never come to understand their real identity in Christ. Their lives are like a flat Coke—no fizz and no fun. But you're different. You definitely don't want to be like that. And this book will help you understand truth that will keep the fizz in your walk with God.

Like never before, you'll dive into the Word and uncover a heart full of treasure. Through Scripture, you'll enter God's Fort Knox of spiritual riches and tour His vault of blessings for you. You'll see who God says you are and how your beliefs dramatically impact your behavior. And you'll find that who you believe you are is who you will eventually become.

Bottom line? Don't wait another minute to make the life-changing discovery of who you really are in Christ. It's a *Done Deal!*

Jeff Kinley

How to Use This Bible Study

To get started, you will need a Bible, this disciple's journal, a pencil, and if you'd like, a notebook.

To begin with, you will find that there is usually an intriguing activity or story to spark your interest in completing this Bible study. Have fun with it, but don't stop there because you will make some exciting discoveries about your relationship with God when you keep going.

You will find that some, but not all, of the Scripture verses are printed here for you. We try to print a passage whenever you are asked to mark it up by underlining, circling words, etc. However, we strongly encourage you to use your own Bible as you work through these studies. We use the New International Version and you should too, if possible. However, feel free to use whatever translation you are most comfortable with.

There is space for you to write down responses to the questions. If you find that you want more room to express yourself, write additional thoughts in some kind of notebook that will be easy to tote with you to the group Bible study. Make sure that your notations are complete enough to make sense to you during the small group Bible study time. You may want to write down key words to spark your memory or you may need to write out complete thoughts—whichever works best for you.

There is also room to express yourself on the "Pray About It" page. Write your personal conversations with God. Talk to Him about, well, anything. Keep track of your requests and God's answers.

Whatever you do, always try to complete the entire week's study before your small group meeting, so that you can get the most out of other people's comments. This way, you won't miss out by trying to catch up on your reading during the small group time.

What Has Christ Done for Me?

Someone has said, "The Bible is like a will—you read it to discover the riches that have been left to you."

Well, if that's true, then you had better brace yourself. Because as we say in the South, you're fixin' to become a spiritual millionaire.

This first unit will help you understand your position in Christ—your standing before Him. It will answer the question, "How does God see me?" Beginning with His creation of you, you'll see how God drew you to Himself and established you in a personal relationship to Him. Through these first five weeks, your real identity in Christ will begin to unfold before your very eyes.

WEEK 1 Image Is Everything

Your Creation in God's Image

My Identity: I am valuable to God.

1 "Elementary, Watson"

He was the most famous and brilliant detective of all time. No, not Inspector Clouseau or Dick Tracy, but another fictional character, Sherlock Holmes. Living in nineteenth-century England, and without modern-day crime-solving technology, Holmes could solve even the most baffling cases of his time. He possessed the ability to walk onto a crime scene and almost immediately uncover what had happened. He could tell when the crime was committed, how it was done, what the criminal was wearing, where the criminal had come from, and what the criminal had eaten for dinner—all in about ten minutes! Holmes would then explain to his ever-present sidekick, Dr. Watson, that the secret of his success was that he had mastered the art of observation. Holmes instinctively knew that at a typical crime scene, the criminal leaves behind many clues and traces—"fingerprints" that reveal much about both the crime and the criminal. Sherlock's genius was in knowing how to look for these "fingerprints."

In a similar way, the Bible says God has left His "fingerprints" all over you—evidence that He has uniquely stamped His mark on you. All you have to do is know how to look for these clues. This first session will help you do a little detective work in your Bible. In it, you'll uncover and understand more clearly the truth about what God really thinks about you. That, in turn, will cause you to see yourself as you truly are.

But before you dive into the deep end, complete the following exercise, choosing the three statements that best describe what influences your view of yourself.

My opinion of myself is largely influenced by . . .

___ what I look like in the mirror.
___ others' opinions of me.
___ society's values.
✳ my talents.
___ what hangs in my closet.
✳ my grades at school.
___ my weaknesses.
___ my ability to be "in" with the right crowd.
___ my attractiveness to the opposite sex.
___ my possessions.
___ my athletic achievements.
✳ what my parents say to me.
✳ what God says about me.
✳ other volunteer work

Put a star beside the ones that you think will really matter to you ten years from now.

2 A Better Idea

Back in the 1920s, a young businessman was driving his Model T Ford down a dusty country road when the car unexpectedly broke down. Not knowing what to do, the young man sat dejected and frustrated on the side of the road. Soon he spotted another Model T in the distance coming toward him. The car stopped, and out stepped a man in an expensive suit. The man calmly walked over, lifted up the hood, took a look inside, connected a loose wire, and started the car. The young businessman couldn't believe his eyes. "How did you know how to do that?" he asked. "Simple," the stranger replied. "I know everything about Model T's. My name is Henry Ford. I invented this car."

When you think about it, it only makes sense to allow the One who created ("invented") us to tell us the truth about ourselves—about what's really "under the hood." It's only then that we can have an accurate view of who we really are.

Genesis 1:26, 27
Then God said, "Let us make man in our image, in our likeness." . . .
So God created man in his own image, in the image of God he created . . . them.

1. What does God say about you in these verses?

2. What do you think that means?

3. What makes you different and distinct from the animals God created?

4. According to Psalm 8:5-8, where exactly are you in God's created order?

Many Bible scholars say having the image of God in us means that we have a moral nature, and that we have intellect, emotion, and choice—like God does.

3 A Tear in the Fabric

In the beginning, humans enjoyed perfect, unbroken fellowship with their Creator. They lived in a perfect environment, a genuine paradise. Adam and Eve were the most beautiful people on earth. (OK, they were the *only* ones.) They reflected God's image accurately. It was a good day in the neighborhood.

1. But something happened that changed all of that—something that marred God's image in Adam and Eve . . . and in us. What was it? (See Genesis 3:1-7.)

2. In what ways do you suppose the image of God in us was altered when Adam and Eve sinned?

4 Your Personal Price Tag

When God saved you through Christ, He began the process of restoring His likeness and image in you (Colossians 3:10). Now you can begin to understand and accept your true worth to God. In fact, every person has a basic need to see his or her personal significance as coming from God.

1. Look up the following verses and write down the reasons given why God says you are so valuable to Him.

- Psalm 139:1-6, 13-17; Jeremiah 1:4, 5

I am valuable because God . . .

- Isaiah 43:1-4

I am valuable because God . . .

- Romans 5:8

I am valuable because God . . .

- Ephesians 1:3

I am valuable because God . . .

• II Corinthians 5:17

I am valuable because God . . .

2. Do you normally think of yourself as having this kind of worth? Why or why not?

It is said that . . .

• *Longfellow* could take a worthless sheet of paper, write a poem on it, and make it worth $6,000.

• *Uncle Sam* can take paper, stamp an emblem on it, and make it worth $1,000.

• *Picasso* could take a 50-cent piece of canvas, paint a picture on it, and make it worth $10,000.

• *Rockefeller* could sign his name to a piece of paper and make it worth $1,000,000.

However, *God* can take you and me, created in His image, send His Son to die for us, and convince us that we are not worthless, but priceless!

Hard to believe? Maybe. But it's true, and you can bank on it!

3. What does knowing your true value to God cause you to feel toward Him? Write your thoughts down.

KEEP In Mind

Think of it. If you were a mere accident of nature, you would have no real worth. But now you know that you are the intimate creation of a loving God. His personal signature is in you as a Christian. You have been created in His image and showered with infinite, eternal love. Because of this, God places the highest possible value on you. Yes, *you!* You are important to Him. And you can't be replaced, because you're one of a kind.

Look back to the statements at the beginning of this session regarding the ways people gain their significance. How does your attitude toward those things change now that you've seen yourself from God's point of view? Would you change any of your top three choices now? If so, which one(s)?

PRAY About It

Close by praying a prayer like the one below as your response to God.

Father, help me to allow the truth of Your Word—not people, things, or circumstances—to determine what I think of myself. And Lord, I praise You that I am valuable and significant to You. Help me live in a way that reflects Your image and character in me. In Jesus' name. Amen.

WEEK 2 Lost and Found

Your Conviction, Calling, and Conversion

My Identity: I am saved by God.

1 Warning Signs

While watching one of those "rescue safety" programs on TV one night, I saw the story of a family who was awakened in the middle of the night by the piercing sound of a smoke alarm. Without hesitation, both mom and dad jumped out of bed, dropped to the floor, and began crawling "commando-style" down the long hall to their children's bedroom. After grabbing the kids, they made a mad dash for the nearest outside door. Standing in the front yard, shaken but relieved, the entire family watched as their home burned to the ground. And though they lost everything they owned, they still had each other, and for that they were grateful. They owed their lives to the shrill warning of a little smoke alarm. It had served as a wake-up call to them that something was very wrong in the house.

Our bodies are equipped with a similar alarm called "pain." That's why, when you go to the doctor, he or she normally asks, "Where does it hurt?" The doctor knows that pain is your body's built-in warning system telling you that something is wrong. If it weren't for pain, your body would be in bad shape! Like that smoke alarm, it may be annoying, but it could save your life!

Now for a little test. Choose the best answer.

1. A pain in your *head* is normally a sign that . . .
    a. you have a headache.
    b. your baseball cap is too tight.
    c. you're studying too hard.
    d. an old lady just slugged you with her purse.

2. A pain in your *stomach* is normally a sign that . . .
    a. you have indigestion.
    b. the revenge of the school cafeteria chili is on its way.
    c. you've just been handed your SAT scores.
    d. you shouldn't have literally "smoked" that turkey for Thanksgiving.

3. A pain in your *tooth* is normally a sign that . . .
    a. you probably have a cavity.
    b. last night's popcorn is still there.
    c. last week's popcorn is still there.
    d. you now know why they call it "rock" candy.

4. A pain in your *ear* is normally a sign that . . .
    a. you may have an ear infection.
    b. you've been on the phone too long.
    c. your best friend's new speakers work better than expected.
    d. you have enough wax in there to start your own museum.

2 Detect-a-Sin

Have you ever gone through a "metal detector" booth at an airport? This beeping device is designed to keep people from transporting concealed weapons onto a plane. Centuries ago, a similar device was already in use. In the palaces of Chang-an, in ancient Thailand, gates were made of lodestone, a natural magnet. If someone tried to sneak through with a concealed dagger, the lodestone would pull at the weapon, causing the individual to reach for it. The palace guards, watching every movement, would then grab the invader.

Similarly, God has installed three primary "sin detectors" in our lives. They're there to "tug" at our hearts, telling us that something is wrong in our lives.

What are these three divinely installed detectors and how do they work? Locate one in each of the following three verses.

Romans 2:15
Since they show that the requirements of the law are written on their hearts, their consciences also bearing witness, and their thoughts now accusing, now even defending them.

• _____

1. In what ways does this inner part of you tell you right from wrong?

Someone has defined the conscience as "the inner voice that warns us somebody may be looking."

Hebrews 4:12
For the word of God is living and active. Sharper than any double-edged sword, it penetrates even to dividing soul and spirit, joints and marrow; it judges the thoughts and attitudes of the heart.

• _____

2. Put in your own words what the Bible can do in your life, according to this verse.

John 16:8
When he [the Holy Spirit] comes, he will convict the world of guilt in regard to sin and righteousness and judgment.

• _____

3. When someone is convicted of a crime in a court of law, what does that mean?

4. How is being convicted of a crime similar to what the Holy Spirit does in us? (See Romans 3:23; 6:23.)

Step One in receiving salvation is recognizing your need for Christ. This happens when God convicts you of your sin. But what exactly is God trying to accomplish by placing this awareness in our lives? Does He get a kick out of telling us what sinners we are? Does He enjoy making us feel guilty? Just what is the purpose in causing us to know that we are sinful?

3 Calling All Sinners

Growing up, you hear your name called a lot. Sometimes that's good and sometimes that's not-so-good. Looking at the following examples, circle the ones that you would look forward to and cross out the ones you would dread.

Your name is called by . . .

• your English teacher just after class.
• your mom at dinner time—and she uses your full name.
• your dad on Saturday morning as he's holding a rake in his hand.
• your dad on Saturday night when you're home two hours past curfew.
• Uncle Sam!
• the good-looking girl or guy at school you've been wanting to date.
• the not-so-good-looking guy or girl at school you've been avoiding.

- your boyfriend or girlfriend after a Friday night out.
- your boyfriend or girlfriend's parents after a Friday night out.
- the police officer who just pulled you over.
- the judges at a talent contest.
- the recruiting scout at your favorite college.
- your boss at the burger joint.
- your big brother whose CDs are missing.
- a big nurse at the doctor's office.
- Ed McMahon from Publishers Clearinghouse.
- representatives of the NBA, NFL, and MLB.
- representatives of the CIA, FBI, and KGB.

Would God ever personally call out your name? If He did, what would He want? Would He be angry? Would you be in trouble? Would He be like a disappointed coach? How would you know it was Him?

You'll be relieved to know that when Jesus called people to Himself in the Gospels, He was inviting them to something wonderful and life changing.

1. What did Jesus call people to in the following verses?

- Matthew 4:17

- Matthew 4:21, 22

- Matthew 11:28-30

• Mark 2:17

• I Peter 2:9

2. Describe how each of the previous passages is a picture of what it means to become a Christian.

3. Why do you suppose some people would view God's call to salvation as a negative thing?

4 | I Once Was Lost . . .

We've seen that when we become Christians, God first convicts us of sin and our need for Christ. That's Step One. The second step is when He issues a personal call to each one of us to come to Him for salvation. But the final step is the best one of all. Here, we actually get to *experience* salvation.

1. Have you ever wondered just what God saves you *from*? Write down some of your thoughts below.

Now read Luke 15:11-32.

2. Taking a fresh look at this familiar parable, jot down how the following aspects of salvation are described there.

- *Your need* for salvation (15:13-16)

- *Your role* in salvation (15:17-20a)

- *God's willingness* to save you (15:20b)

- *God's part* in your salvation (15:22-24)

It's a staggering thought to realize that God is more willing to come to us than we are to come to Him! (For a further illustration of this, see Luke 15:1-10.)

Ephesians 2:8, 9
For it is by grace you have been saved, through faith—and this not from yourselves,
it is the gift of God—not by works, so that no one can boast.

3. How does a person receive God's salvation?

4. What does "faith" mean?

5. Can you think of an illustration of this kind of saving faith in everyday life?

6. Do you remember when you put your faith in Christ for salvation? (It's OK if you can't remember the exact date. It's just important that you are certain you have trusted Christ.)

7. Complete the following sentences:

• The most vivid memory I have of becoming a Christian is . . .

• Since Christ came into my life, some of the ways He has changed me include . . .

Several years back, our nation paused to follow the story of a little two-year-old Midland, Texas, girl who had become lost in her own backyard. After looking for her without success, her mother heard cries of help coming from—of all places—the ground! Little Jessica McClure had fallen into a tiny well in her backyard. Trapped and in pain for hours, doctors feared for her life as work crews labored in a heroic effort to rescue the little girl. The whole town, along with the entire nation, gathered to watch. News reporters from every major network came to carefully monitor every bit of the story.

As the hours passed, Jessica's mother would periodically get on her knees and sing Jessica's favorite bedtime songs to bring comfort to her hurting daughter. This story was a headline of a different kind—not a headline of crime, but a headline of hope. Earthmovers, digging equipment, construction workers, and medical teams from all over the area worked around the clock. They did whatever it took to save her. No price was too high, no sacrifice too great, for a little girl's life was at stake. Finally, after hours of digging, scraping, cutting, and praying, rescue workers gently lifted Jessica's bruised and battered little body out of that well. The hundreds of people who had gathered around the yard shed tears of joy and erupted with cheers and applause. It was perhaps the most emotional moment of the year for our nation. Why? Because little Jessica was saved. She was going to be all right.

Friend, God did all that for you and much more. He came looking for you when you were lost. He heard your cries for help. He found you in your sin and spared no expense, moving heaven and earth just to rescue you. That's how much He cared. As you read and study through the chapters in this book, you will discover even more incredible things that God has done for you. In doing so, your desire to know and love God will grow to a new level. So press on!

In order for you to come to Christ, you had to know that you truly needed Him. And for that to happen, God had to show you that need by convicting you of sin through His Word. But He didn't leave you there under the pile. (Aren't you glad?) He wanted a relationship with you so badly that He lovingly called you to Himself. Once this happened, your part was simply to put your faith in Jesus to save you.

PRAY About It

Let this section serve as a place to jot down what's going on in your life right now. What can you praise God for? What do you need to ask Him for? What do you need to thank Him for? Write down your prayers and prayer requests and keep a record of God's faithfulness.

Using the earlier illustration, imagine that you're Jessica McClure. What would you want to say to those who rescued you? Now transfer those thoughts and feelings into a prayer of praise and thanksgiving to God for saving you.

WEEK 3 You're Right!

Your Justification before God

My Identity: I am righteous and holy.

1 Kids, Don't Try This at Home

On July 19, 1994, Susan Williams of Fresno, California, stuck a wad of gum in her mouth and became the world's biggest bubble blower. She blew a beach-ball-sized bubble measuring a record twenty-three inches.

And speaking of mouths, Bobbie Sherlock and Ray Blanzina, of Pittsburgh, Pennsylvania, once held the record for the longest kiss ever. According to the *Guinness Book of Records*, they locked lips from May 1 to 7, 1978, for an unbelievable 130 hours and 2 minutes! Talk about a super smack! That's a mega "mouth-to-mouth"! Can you imagine the chapped lips? the bad breath? And what would you say to someone after a kiss like that? "Thanks. I had a good time. Call me sometime. Goodnight"?

Imagine what would happen if you combined the bubble-blowing girl with the kissing guy—never mind.

OK, enough of the improbable. Which of the following things do you think you are *actually* capable of? Which would be impossible for you to achieve?

- Maintain a 4.0 gradepoint this semester.
- Go for a full year without getting a traffic ticket.
- Go for two weeks without a burger or pizza.
- Make the athletic team of your choice at school.
- Leap tall buildings in a single bound.
- Have three good hair days in a row.
- Please your boss at work.
- Have perfect church attendance for six months.
- Drink a Coke without burping.
- Swim the English Channel.
- Have a date every weekend for ten straight weeks.
- Go for seven days without watching sports on TV.
- Get up on time for school every day for three weeks.
- Run a mile in under six minutes.
- Attain perfection before God.

Some of these things do seem impossible—especially going without burgers and pizza!

2 Members Only

As mere mortals, there are thousands of impossible feats that are way out of our reach. And for some of the ones listed previously, it's really no big deal. (Who really wants to go without watching sports on TV anyway?) But when it comes to being perfect before God, it really is a big deal. In fact, it's the most important thing in this life—as well as the next. Let's find out why.

1. When you think about heaven (and you will in Week 15 of this study), do you ever wonder who will be there? What groups of people will and won't go to heaven?

I Corinthians 6:9-11
Do you not know that the wicked will not inherit the kingdom of God? Do not be deceived: Neither the sexually immoral nor idolaters nor adulterers nor male prostitutes nor homosexual offenders nor thieves nor the greedy nor drunkards nor slanderers nor swindlers will inherit the kingdom of God. And that is what some of you were. But you were washed, you were sanctified, you were justified in the name of the Lord Jesus Christ and by the Spirit of our God.

2. Why would God exclude some people from heaven, yet accept others? (See Hebrews 12:14.)

3. If God demands 100% perfection and holiness, that rules us out, doesn't it? And since we've already previously botched that perfection, where does that leave us? (See John 3:18.)

4. Take sixty seconds to brainstorm ways in which people still try to make themselves "good enough" for heaven.

3 The Great Exchange

What's your favorite foreign language? Spanish? German? French? Russian? Italian? Thousand Island? How about Chinese? One reason Chinese is so hard to learn is that it is made up of *characters* instead of letters. In fact, there are some 40,000 characters in the Chinese language! Because of this, the Chinese language is very colorful and picturesque. This is especially true when it comes to the Chinese word for *righteousness.* The Chinese word is actually composed of two separate characters—one standing for a *lamb,* the other meaning *me.* When "lamb" is placed directly over "me," a new character—*righteousness*—is formed.

I wonder if the Chinese understood the principle of "substitution," of someone suffering for another in his or her place.

John 1:29b
Look, the Lamb of God, who takes away the sin of the world!

1. Why would John refer to Jesus this way?

2. What do you know about the lambs used for sacrifice in Bible times? (See I Peter 1:18, 19.)

3. How did Jesus perfectly fulfill that requirement? (See I Peter 2:22.)

4. Why do you suppose Jesus had to be sinless in order to die for our sins?

Jesus paid the penalty. He suffered and died in our place. The just for the unjust. He was perfect and holy and clean. He never sinned. And the cross now becomes the basis and foundation of our identity before God and our relationship to Him.

4 Becoming a Perfect "10"

In baseball, it's the no-hitter. In bowling, it's the perfect game. In archery, it's the bull's eye. In golf, it's the hole-in-one. And in gymnastics, it's the perfect "10." Every sport has its ultimate standard, the pinnacle of perfection. And few are ever able to attain it. What coach in his or her right mind would demand a perfect score just to make the team?

God does. The difference between sports coaches and God is that God actually *demands* perfection before any of us ever set foot in heaven. But the great news is that when Jesus Christ died on the cross, He accomplished that perfection for you and me.

II Corinthians 5:21
God made him who had no sin to be sin for us, so that in him we might become the righteousness of God.

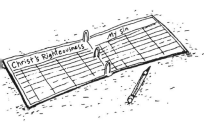

What took place at the cross was a great exchange. You exchanged your sin for the righteousness of the Son of God. And He took on Himself the debt and penalty for all of your sin. In fact, He assumed your sin and was punished by God for it. Because of that sacrifice, the Bible says you can now be "justified." We may treat this word as an accounting term. Think of two columns in a ledger. Written in one column is Christ's righteousness and in the other column is your sin. God, the Divine Accountant, erases your sin and replaces it with the holiness of Christ Himself! You possess Jesus' righteousness! You are accepted as being as holy as He is, and God declares you forever "not guilty"!

What are some of the incredible benefits of being justified in God's sight?

• Romans 5:9; 8:1

I have no fear of . . .

• Ephesians 1:4

In God's sight, I am . . .

• Hebrews 10:14

My right standing before God will last . . .

• I John 3:7

Because God has declared me righteous, I am now able to . . .

KEEP In Mind

My wife Beverly and I were married in a magnificent old cathedral in downtown Little Rock, Arkansas. And though I have scores of memories of that beautiful spring day, the most vivid memory in my mind occurred at the beginning of the ceremony. The groomsmen and bridesmaids had all come forward. There we stood at the front of the cathedral, my pastor on my right and my dad on my left. The music paused for a second, and then with a mighty blast of those massive pipes the organist burst into playing "Trumpet Voluntary." The back doors of the building swung open and there stood Beverly with her dad. She was dressed in the wedding gown her mother had worn thirty years before; yet it was perfectly preserved, white and spotless. The congregation rose at once to its feet in honor of the bride. All attention was now focused on her. Meanwhile, up front, I was choking back the tears as a watermelon-sized lump formed in my throat. And the thought that kept repeating over and over in my mind was *God, she is so beautiful, so innocent and pure. Jesus, thank You that one day, I will be presented to You just as she is presented to me—spotless, pure, and righteous—Your righteous bride.*

Get this: God declares a Christian's position before Him right now to be the same as it will be on that day—righteous, holy, spotless, blameless, pure, pleasing, and acceptable to the Lord! And remember, this righteous standing came through faith in Christ, not by any good works that you have done (Romans 4:2-5).

PRAY About It

Spend some time praying through the four benefits of justification you discovered on page 34. Then turn to personal requests for the week ahead. Don't forget to record updates on answered prayer.

WEEK 4 Cease Fire!

Your Reconciliation in Christ

Hey!
Wanna
hear 'bout
Jesus..?

My Identity: I am a friend of God.

1 Tora! Tora! Tora!

While in college, I spent a summer with fifty other students living in Hawaii as a missionary. (Hey, somebody's got to reach those people!) While there, apart from the thrill and beauty of body surfing and witnessing on the beach, I was struck with the awesome history of that tiny group of islands. Right there on Oahu, some forty years earlier, Japanese planes had come streaking across the sky on a sleepy Sunday morning in December. They were on their way to bomb America's unsuspecting Pacific fleet, anchored in Pearl Harbor. While there, I stood on the mountains that overlooked the valley those planes flew through on their final bombing approach. I imagined Japanese Zeros with young pilots crying out, "Tora! Tora! Tora!" ("Attack!") as they made their way into one of the most unforgettable moments in history. Shortly after this attack, the United States officially declared war on Japan. And for the next four years, we were engaged in a global conflict.

All you have to do is pick up the daily paper to discover that somewhere in the world, there is a war, battle, or revolution going on in some country or nation.

Bringing this theme a little closer to home, how do you see "wars" around you in . . .

- society?

- the streets?

- the family?

- the government?

- marriage?

- friendships?

2 Rebel with a Lost Cause

The Bible says that before we knew Christ as our Savior, we too were in a war. But our enemy wasn't some country halfway across the world. Our battle-ground was in our own heart! We were enemies with God because, inwardly, we had rebelled against Him.

1. Before coming to know Christ, what was our heart attitude toward God? (See Romans 8:7.)

Colossians 1:21
Once you were alienated from God and were enemies
in your minds because of your evil behavior.

2. What do you think is the relationship between being an enemy of God and our former evil behavior?

3. According to James 4:4, what is another reason we were enemies of God?

4. What images normally come to mind when you think of hating someone?

5. What did our hatred of God look like in our lives? (See Romans 1:29-31.)

You may not have felt like you actually hated God before you became a Christian, especially if you came to Christ as a child. But the Bible indicates that our hatred was there in our nature, our attitudes, and our actions. Our sinful nature is like a wild horse—rebellious, unwilling to be tamed or broken.

It runs from the idea of someone else being in control. And our attitudes follow our nature. They're self-centered, self-serving, proud, and obedient to our own desires instead of God's. But we also demonstrate a hatred of God with our actions—including gossip, putting others down, acting unloving toward others, lying, and disobeying our parents.

In our war with God, it was only a matter of time before we would ultimately lose. And the personal casualties we would suffer in this life and the next were a price too high to pay. We needed peace. So God brought peace.

3 Peace Treaty

Have you ever gotten in a fight or had someone mad at you? Maybe as a child it was the neighborhood bully or an older sibling. More recently it could've been your parents, your best friend, your boyfriend or girlfriend. But then you talk things out and make things right between the two of you. There are few things in life better than a restored relationship. That's exactly what happened when you became a Christian (Colossians 1:21, 22). Your personal war with God officially ended. Peace was declared at Christ's cross. And now you get to enjoy all of the blessings that come from that restored relationship. Looking up the verses that follow, find out what came to you when Jesus made peace with God on your behalf.

Romans 5:1
Therefore, since we have been justified through faith,
we have peace with God through our Lord Jesus Christ.

1. What did you get when you received Christ?

2. Describe another benefit of reconciliation found in John 14:27 and Philippians 4:7.

3. What do you think is the difference between peace *with* God and the peace *of* God?

- Romans 5:10

- Ephesians 2:11-16

II Corinthians 5:18-20
All this is from God, who reconciled us to himself through Christ and gave us the ministry of reconciliation: that God was reconciling the world to himself in Christ, not counting men's sins against them. And he has committed to us the message of reconciliation. We are therefore Christ's ambassadors, as though God were making his appeal through us. We implore you on Christ's behalf: Be reconciled to God.

4. What did God do after He reconciled us to Himself?

5. What do you think the following words mean in these verses?
- *gave*

- *committed*

- *ambassadors*

6. What are some ways you can effectively represent Christ to your world?

KEEP In Mind

The entire world had waited and prayed for this moment. Finally, on September 2, 1945, Japan formally surrendered to the United States aboard the aircraft carrier *USS Missouri* in Tokyo Bay. Flanked by his military leaders, the Japanese foreign minister signed a document of unconditional surrender in the presence of United States General Douglas MacArthur. When the ink of the last signature had dried, World War II was officially over. Back home in America, all across the country, people began to dance and celebrate in the streets, crying tears of joy. Why? Because peace for them meant husbands and fathers and sons were at last coming home. Because the war was over, relationships they longed for would finally be restored. They would be together again.

When Jesus bore our sin on the cross, He signed the peace treaty between God and man in His own blood. The war is now officially over! Chisel this fact forever into your heart and mind—God isn't angry with you. Jesus satisfied God's wrath toward your sin. You are now among God's closest friends (John 15:15)! He wants you to now enjoy all of the benefits of reconciliation—peace with Him, peace from Him, joy, peace with others, and the privilege of telling unbelievers about Him. Are you enjoying these blessings?

PRAY About It

Take a quick glance back at the heart attitude you listed in Section II on page 39. Do any of these currently threaten your "peace factor" from time to time? Spend some time in prayer focusing on the friendship and peace you now have with God. Then ask the Lord to guard you from those specific heart attitudes that would prevent you from experiencing His peace daily.

Lock, Stock, and Barrel

Your Redemption in Christ

My Identity: I am freed from sin, Satan, and the Law.

1 A Ransom for Handsome

It's not easy being young these days. The pressure to fit in, sell out, and live up to the world's expectations can be overwhelming at times. And the things that happen to you as a teenager are things that mark you for life. Such was the case of Jean Paul Getty III. As a young man, he never worried about "fitting in." His good looks and charm made him instantly popular with the crowd. On top of that, his grandfather was oil billionaire Jean Paul Getty, one of the richest men in the world. But all the fun and popularity that comes with that kind of wealth faded fast one day when young Jean Paul was kidnapped by Italian terrorists. His grandfather at first refused to pay the ransom. But he quickly changed his mind when the kidnappers sent him his grandson's ear in the mail! (Yuck!) The billionaire promptly paid the ransom of $750,000 and got his grandson back again.

2 The Worst Kind of Slavery

Though the Bible never says we were "kidnapped," it does say that before we came to Christ, we were held captive and imprisoned. And like young Jean Paul, we desperately needed someone to pay the ransom and obtain our release. We needed a redeemer. To redeem means to free someone or to buy him or her back by paying a ransom or a penalty.

To fully appreciate our spiritual redemption, we must first understand the extent of our slavery and what held us captive.

John 8:34
Jesus replied, "I tell you the truth, everyone who sins is a slave to sin."

1. Would you call this a spiritual principle? Why or why not?

2. Another former "spiritual master" over you was _____ . (See Acts 26:17, 18 and Colossians 1:13.)

3. What else kept you in bondage? (See Ephesians 2:1, 2.)

4. Look up Galatians 4:1-5. Summarize the big idea in these verses.

5. What rights do you suppose a slave had in Bible times? Explain your answer.

6. In what way did your old "masters" have the same authority over you?

3 The Royal Redeemer

Once we recognize how great our need for redemption really is, we discover that just like a slave, we have no prospect for escape from this bondage. And though many religions also recognize that humans have this problem, not one of them offers a bonified redeemer. That's what makes Christianity unique. Jesus is the Redeemer.

So what made Christ the perfect Redeemer for us? To find the answer, we have to refer back to the Book of Ruth. Back then, God made provision for slaves to be set free if certain conditions were met. The person seeking to free a slave had to meet four basic requirements. Let's see what they are and how Jesus met all of them for us.

As you look up the following verses, write down the four ways Jesus qualified to be your perfect Redeemer.

CONDITION #1

He must be a *relative* of the one needing redemption (Leviticus 25:47-49; Ruth 3:12, 13).

• JESUS MEETS IT (Hebrews 2:14, 15).

1. In what sense is Jesus "related" to you?

CONDITION #2

He must be *able* to pay the price (Ruth 4:4-6).

• JESUS MEETS IT (I Peter 1:18, 19).

2. Complete this sentence: Jesus is worthy to redeem me because . . .

CONDITION #3

He must be *willing* to redeem (Ruth 4:4-6).

• JESUS MEETS IT (John 10:17, 18; Luke 22:42).

3. How was Jesus' willingness to redeem you tested?

CONDITION #4

He must *not need* redemption himself. (It would make sense that if you were a slave, you were in no position to purchase someone else out of slavery.)

• JESUS MEETS IT (Hebrews 4:15).

4. Why didn't Jesus need redemption Himself?

Jesus—and only Jesus—is the perfect Redeemer for humankind.

4 Property of Jesus

What real difference does redemption make in your life today, this week, and for the rest of your life? One way you can look at it is to see how it has changed your relationship to your former "masters." Find the verses listed below in your Bible and complete the sentences.

Because Christ has redeemed me . . .

• I am freed from being in bondage to _____ (Galatians 3:13).

• I am no longer enslaved to _____ (Titus 2:14).

• I am fully released from slavery to _____ (Romans 6:16-18).

• I am forever delivered from the power of _____ (Acts 26:18; Colossians 1:13, 14).

1. Read I Corinthians 6:19, 20. In what sense would you say you are now a "slave of God"?

2. Why doesn't being Christ's servant have a negative connotation? (See I John 5:3.)

3. What is another natural response to God in light of your redemption? (See Revelation 5:9.)

You see, Jesus broke your chains. He ripped the door to your spiritual jail right off its hinges. You are now free to get up and follow the One who gave His life as payment to release you.

There was a young boy who lived in a New England seaport and loved to watch the boats come in from their daily catch. One day he decided to build a little sailboat of his own. He worked for weeks, making sure each detail was just right. Finally, the big day arrived. He went down to the wharf and proudly put his boat in the water. As he triumphantly watched his new sailboat, he noticed that the wind had suddenly changed, and the tiny boat was being swept out of sight. The little boy was heartbroken. Each day for a month he went back to see if his boat had been washed up on shore, but he left each time discouraged and disappointed.

Finally, one day he saw his boat in a nearby store window. He excitedly burst into the store and explained his story to the owner. But she responded by saying that the boat would now cost him two dollars. After pleading with the owner to no effect, the boy reached into his pocket, pulled out all of the money he had—two dollars—and gave it to the store owner. As he was leaving the store, he said, "Little boat, you are twice mine. You are mine because I made you, and now you are mine because I bought you."

Jesus says to you today, "My child, you are twice mine. You are mine because I made you, and now you are mine because I bought you. I did all of this because I love you." (See Ephesians 1:5, 9, 11.)

KEEP In Mind

The phrase "lock, stock, and barrel" dates back to the time of the American Revolution. Those three items were the essential components of a gun—the barrel, the stock, and the lock (or firing mechanism). In other words, it was a way of saying "the entire gun, the whole thing, every part of it."

What about you? Does God own you "lock, stock, and barrel"? Do you see yourself as belonging to Him? Do you acknowledge that your life is not your own? Do you recognize Him as your Master? Are you obeying Him? Are you submitting your desires to Him? Is there an area of your life over which you have yet to give Him ownership? If so, write it down and give it over to Him right now in prayer.

PRAY About It

Lord, I recognize that You have bought me with a great price—Your own life. I know I belong to You and acknowledge You as being worthy to be my Master. I count it an honor to be Your slave. Thank You for rescuing me from sin, Satan, and the curse of the Law. I praise You that while I was on the auction block, You bid for me and bought me with Your own blood. For that, I ask You to direct every part of me today. I love You and I joyfully serve You with my life. Amen.

UNIT Two

What Has Christ Done in Me?

So far, you've learned some pretty incredible things about yourself (if you're a Christian) that you may not have known before—things that may totally change the way you look at God, yourself, and life. You've seen that God has created you in His image and declared you righteous in His sight. You've been reconciled to God and are no longer His enemy, but His friend. You've been redeemed and bought out of slavery to sin. And you've been adopted as God's precious child and brought into His family with all of the full status and rights of an adult son or daughter.

Doesn't knowing these things begin to give you a whole new outlook on your salvation and relationship to God? It's kind of like the little boy's description of an elevator: "I got into this little room and the upstairs came down!" You could say, "I'm getting into these truths and heaven's coming down!"

But what else could God possibly do for us? How much better can it get?

The good news is that the good news gets even better! Truth is, you've only just begun to scratch the surface of the riches in your spiritual bank vault. As you continue now to look at who you are in Christ, you will gain a biblical perspective on everything from yourself to life in general. You'll look at your new life in Christ, your adoption in God's family, your access to God, your identification with His church, and the assurance of your salvation.

So keep your seat belt buckled, because there's more to come. It actually does get better! This section will introduce you to yet another facet of who you are in Christ.

Fresh Start

Your New Life in Christ

My Identity: I am alive in Christ.

1 Get the Point?

Maybe you've heard of the man who went to his psychiatrist claiming that he was dead. The psychiatrist spent many sessions trying every approach imaginable to convince the man that he was alive, but with no success. Nothing seemed to be working. Finally, he asked the man, "Do you believe that dead men bleed?" The disturbed man replied, "Of course not. Everybody knows that dead men don't bleed!" And with that, the psychiatrist took a needle and pricked the man's finger, causing it to bleed. "See there," said the psychiatrist, "now what does that tell you?" The disturbed man exclaimed, "Well, what do you know. Dead men do bleed after all!"

A bleeding dead man is sort of like an oxymoron (no, that's not an ox with an I.Q. of 50). An oxymoron refers to two or more words that seem to contradict one another. For example:

• Jumbo shrimp
• Black light
• Cold hot tamale
• Low-fat dessert

- Dead live oak
- Freezer burn
- Military intelligence

Can you come up with a few of your own?

- _____
- _____
- _____
- _____

Oxymorons just don't seem to make sense, do they? Here are a few others that sound even more insane:

- Dead church
- Boring Bible study
- Lukewarm Christian

Now those are words that should never be found together in the same sentence. Yet sadly, they are too often an accurate description of some churches, Bible studies, and Christians. In fact, there are people claiming to know Christ who are walking around like the living dead. They appear to be "Christian corpses." It's sometimes hard to tell whether these people have just come from a Bible study or from a funeral! There's just no excitement in them. No aliveness. No spiritual passion. Nothing that says, "I'm alive in Christ!" They're like the tombstone that reads, "Died at 30. Buried at 70." They truly are the "walking dead."

But the Bible describes Christians in a very different way—in fact, as just the opposite of this. God says that believers are very much alive in Him. But what does that mean? And how do we prevent ourselves from becoming like those "Christian cadavers"? The answer is found in understanding and experiencing the new life God gave you in Jesus Christ.

2 Nic at Nite

Read John 3:1-15.

A little background info would help us here. We know that Nicodemus was a Pharisee and a very good moral and religious man. He fasted two days every week. He spent two hours a day in prayer at the temple and tithed all of his income. He memorized large sections of Scripture regularly. It was as if he taught theology at the local seminary. He was one of Israel's foremost religious leaders. And he was very sincere in his faith. Quite a religious resumé, huh? How many of us carry those kinds of credentials? If anyone was a candidate for heaven, Nicodemus was. Or was he?

1. What was Jesus' counsel to him? (3:3)

2. Why do you think Nicodemus totally missed the point here? (3:4)

3. How does Jesus explain to him what it means to be born again? (3:5-8)

Have you seen the T-shirt that reads, "Born Once. Die Twice. Born Twice. Die Once"? That's exactly what Jesus was telling Nicodemus. Each of us has to receive and experience a spiritual rebirth in order to enter heaven. And Jesus makes it clear that salvation doesn't come from within us or from the things around us, but rather from above.

3 Salvation in the Cemetery

Each of us had two parents involved in our physical births. God's Word tells us we also have two "parents" responsible for our spiritual births—the Holy Spirit (John 3:8) and the Word of God.

1. According to John 1:12, 13, what three things could never produce spiritual life in you?

2. Why couldn't you just do it yourself? What prevented you?

- Ephesians 2:1

- Romans 3:10-12

- Romans 8:7

Think of it. What did *you* have to do with your physical birth? In the same way, you and I could no more give ourselves spiritual life than a dead man could make himself alive again.

3. Since humans are naturally religious, we are constantly looking for ways to bring life and excitement into our dull world and to change ourselves. Looking at the examples below, circle the ones that you notice the most in your school or community.

Psychology   Sociology

Government programs

Drugs   Dieting   **Meditation**

The occult   New Age philosophies

Being good   Church attendance   **New Year's resolutions**

Turning over a new leaf

Buying new clothes   **Making new friends**

Changing jobs   Sports

Romance   Other: _____

Though some of these could fall into the category of things that may *reform* you, none of them can *transform* you. They can't make you a new person or cause you to possess God's spiritual life. However, God is able to totally transform lives and make them brand new. And that's precisely what He did for you!

4. What part did God's Word play in your new life in Christ? (See I Peter 1:23-25.)

5. Paraphrase the following two Scripture passages in your own words, describing what God did to give you new life in Christ.

Ephesians 2:4, 5
But because of his great love for us, God, who is rich in mercy, made us alive with Christ even when we were dead in transgressions—it is by grace you have been saved.

Titus 3:4, 5
But when the kindness and love of God our Savior appeared, he saved us, not because of righteous things we had done, but because of his mercy. He saved us through the washing of rebirth and renewal by the Holy Spirit.

6. What practical changes does this new birth through the Spirit make in your life?

• II Corinthians 5:17

My character—

- I Peter 1:3

My future—

- I John 3:9

My conduct—

- I John 4:7

My relationships—

- I John 5:4

My victory—

- I John 5:18

My adversary—

Wow! What a difference being born again makes in our lives! How could we ever be lukewarm or apathetic? How could we ever be boring or "dead"? We're alive!

KEEP In Mind

In England, there is a paper factory that makes the finest stationery in the world. One day, a man touring the factory asked what the stationery was made from. He was taken to the very back of the factory and shown a huge pile of dirty rags. "This is what we make our stationery from," he was told. Surprised and somewhat unbelieving, he left the factory. A few weeks later, he received a package in the mail. Opening it, he found a box of beautiful stationery with his initials embossed on it. On the top sheet were written the words "Dirty rags transformed."

Your life isn't "dirty rags" anymore. You've been made brand new, given a new life and a fresh start. You've been born again, from above, by God's Spirit. You're alive in Christ! Your past is forgotten, your present is promising, and your future is full of hope. Enjoy your new life!

PRAY About It

Write a poem built around the contrasts between your old life and your new life in Christ. Then pray that poem back to God in prayer. And don't forget to list your requests for this week.

Once when I was dead, I . . .   *But now that I'm alive in Christ . . .*

WEEK 7 Rags to Riches

Your Adoption as a Child of God

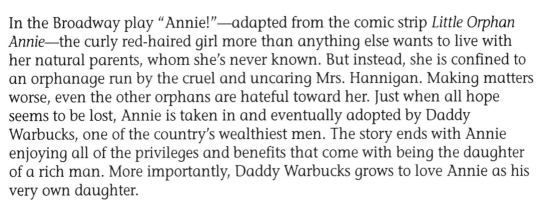

My Identity: I am a child of God.

1 Rich Little Redhead

In the Broadway play "Annie!"—adapted from the comic strip *Little Orphan Annie*—the curly red-haired girl more than anything else wants to live with her natural parents, whom she's never known. But instead, she is confined to an orphanage run by the cruel and uncaring Mrs. Hannigan. Making matters worse, even the other orphans are hateful toward her. Just when all hope seems to be lost, Annie is taken in and eventually adopted by Daddy Warbucks, one of the country's wealthiest men. The story ends with Annie enjoying all of the privileges and benefits that come with being the daughter of a rich man. More importantly, Daddy Warbucks grows to love Annie as his very own daughter.

What a fitting illustration this orphan's story is! It beautifully pictures what takes place in the life of every believer in Jesus Christ. We too have gone from being orphans in a cruel and hopeless world to the enjoyment and warmth of our adoptive Father's care. But have you ever thought about how your adoption changed your relationship with God? How is your relationship with Him different now? What are the advantages of being His child? Take a closer look now to find out what became yours when God adopted you into His family.

1. Describe what it means for a child to be adopted in our modern-day society.

2. What rights and privileges does the child have?

2 Heir Supply

Centuries ago, in the Roman Empire, adopted children had certain special rights and privileges. In his letter to the Christians living in Galatia, the apostle Paul draws from those customs to show us what our relationship with God is like.

Galatians 4:1-5

What I am saying is that as long as the heir is a child, he is no different from a slave, although he owns the whole estate. He is subject to guardians and trustees until the time set by his father. So also, when we were children, we were in slavery under the basic principles of the world. But when the time had fully come, God sent His Son, born of a woman, born under law, to redeem those under law, that we might receive the full rights of sons.

1. According to the last sentence in this paragraph, what is your birthright as a child of God?

2. What do you think "full rights" means?

3. What other privilege comes with being God's adopted child? (See Romans 8:16, 17.)

4. What do you suppose a "co-heir" would be?

5. Read Revelation 21:1-7. Based on these verses, draw a line through the following things that will *not* be a part of your future inheritance.

- A new heaven
- A new earth
- Unlimited video games
- Free pizza
- God's presence
- A million dollars in cash
- A lake house
- God Himself
- A jet ski to ride on the River of Life
- Cable TV
- A pain-free environment
- Eternal life
- Your own condo overlooking New Jerusalem

What's left is part of your future inheritance!

6. What else does God say about this inheritance? (See I Peter 1:3, 4.)

Of course, everyone knows that the value of any child's inheritance is determined by who his or her father is and how much the father owns. Your Father just happens to be the God of the universe! All of the riches of heaven and earth are His! He owns it all. And He has things planned for you that are even beyond your wildest imagination (see I Corinthians 2:9). God has actually written your name into His will through adoption! And though some of that inheritance doesn't become yours until you get to heaven, you still can enjoy full status as an adult child in God's family right now.

Think of your inheritance as a room full of unopened Christmas gifts on Christmas Eve. It won't be long until you'll be able to take full advantage of all that God has to offer you in heaven. So hang in there.

Based on what you've learned so far, what would you say is the best part of your inheritance? Why?

3 The Dad You Never Had

Consider the following "believe it or not" geographical facts:

• The Pacific end of the Panama Canal is further east than the Atlantic end.

• The entire continent of South America lies further east than Florida.

• The island of Cuba would stretch from New York to Chicago.

• You could put 212 Rhode Islands inside the state of Texas.

• Speaking of Texas, the city of Texline, Texas, is closer to the state capitals of Colorado, Kansas, New Mexico, and Oklahoma than it is to its own state's capital, Austin.

And, for your amusement, would you believe the following are actual Southern town names?

• Odd, West Virginia (where folks get even)

• Oil Trough, Arkansas (they have greased pigs)

• Smartt, Tennessee (but can they spell?)

- Peculiar, Missouri (an odd name)

- Normal, Alabama (where is Abnormal?)

- Ninety Six, South Carolina (Ninety Seven is just down the road)

- Sour Lake, Texas (a lemonade lake?)

- Humansville, Missouri (named for the kind of people who live there)

Yes, these are actual towns. Hard to believe?

Now here's something else that may be hard to believe: Because God has adopted you as His child, there is now no limit to how close you can get to Him.

That's right. Your adoption means more than merely being the heir to a future inheritance. God is not like some rich corporate executive who gives his children money, but doesn't ever spend time with them at home. God doesn't demand that His children dress up for dinner and speak to Him only in formal terms. Instead, He allows us to have a special kind of intimacy with Him. He is the perfect Father to us, the Father none of us has ever had. But what does this intimacy look like? We've seen the future aspect of our adoption. But what effect does adoption have on your personal relationship with God?

Galatians 4:6
Because you are sons, God sent the Spirit of his Son into our hearts,
the Spirit who calls out, "Abba, Father."

1. What do you think the word *Abba* means?

2. Why would this be a more endearing term than *Father*?

3. What are some ways that God shows Himself to be a good "Daddy" to you?

  • Psalm 103:13, 14

  • I John 1:3

  • Matthew 7:9-11

4. List a few examples of some of the "good gifts" in your life.

5. Look at Hebrews 12:5-11. Why would this be a great advantage to you?

4 Honoring the Family Name

As teenagers, many of us go through a time when we are "ashamed" of our parents. We walk ten steps in front of them at the mall. We ask to be dropped off down the street from our friends' houses. We prefer that they go out when we have a party at home. Sometimes we're embarrassed about the cars our parents drive. Or we're afraid that if we bring friends home, Dad will start telling them his tired, old, corny jokes. (I'm convinced that my kids will have this fear.) But for the most part, this is simply the awkward way we sometimes try to gain our own identity and independence. In short, we're afraid our friends will see our parents' shortcomings. However, when it comes to our heavenly Father, we have no reason to be ashamed of Him because He has no imperfections.

1. How should we respond to our perfect Parent? What kinds of sons and daughters will we be if we see God as our loving, compassionate, and intimate Daddy?

- I John 5:1-3

- Colossians 1:10

In Bible times, children were taught to live lives worthy of their family names, and to bring honor to them. They understood that they were to avoid anything that would drag those names "through the mud." How much more should we, who have been adopted by the perfect Father, want to live a life pleasing and honoring to Him, since we have been called by His name?

2. In your opinion, how can a Christian keep from dishonoring the name of Christ? Try not to be too vague in your answer.

3. What did Jesus say happens when we live the kind of lifestyle that honors His name? (See Matthew 5:16.)

4. What does that mean?

5. In what ways does your adoption motivate you to love and obey God? Be specific in your answer.

KEEP In Mind

Being adopted goes beyond God, as a righteous judge, declaring you "not guilty." He is more than a Master to you now. He's your Father. Adoption pictures a family, with all of the love a perfect Daddy could give. You are no longer an orphan, but a child with all of the rights and privileges of a full-grown son or daughter. Why did God do all of this? So that you can enjoy your inheritance and spiritual wealth. You have moved from the slaves' quarters to the main house! You have an eternal inheritance. A future. A hope.

Don't you think a Father who would do all of that for you deserves your obedience and loyalty? How will you honor Him more through the way you live? In what ways will you be proud of Him as your Father? How will others see the family likeness in you? Will you remind yourself often of the privileges you now enjoy because you are God's adopted child?

PRAY About It

One of the things you learned in this session was that God wants to give you good gifts and that He knows how to do that as a loving Father. In your closing prayer, talk to Him as though you really believe that He has your best interests at heart. A good verse to guide your prayer time is Jeremiah 29:11.

WEEK 8 No Appointment Necessary

Your Personal Access to God

My Identity: I have gone from isolation to intimacy in my relationship with God.

1 Your Claim to Fame

Several years ago I had the opportunity to take part in the filming of a TV miniseries about the Civil War. For three weeks I went to work on location at an actual Hollywood film set. I saw up close how movies were made and got to dress in authentic uniforms. But the greatest thrill of all was in meeting famous actors. Each day, I would go to a trailer on the set where I would sit beside famous people while we went through make-up together. I even got to talk to some of them. When the miniseries finally aired on TV, I ended up in a grand total of three scenes playing three different characters! (OK, they were small, nonspeaking roles, but it was still a big deal for me!)

Have you ever met anyone famous—someone you could call your "claim to fame"? Perhaps a pro athlete? Or an actor? a musician? a Christian speaker? a politician? your uncle Morty, the local bowling champ? Write down the name of that person.

• I've actually met _____ in person.

• Complete this statement: "If I could spend ten minutes with anyone in the world, it would be _____ ."

What would prevent you from fulfilling that dream?

How would your chances improve if you knew someone close to that person (a manager, relative, friend, fellow celebrity, etc.)?

2 The Thrill Is Gone

It would be great to know someone famous, wouldn't it? But after a while, the thrill might begin to wear off a little. You might even start taking that person for granted, like it was no big deal to know him or her. In reality, we take a lot of things for granted in our lives. For example, think of the conveniences we have that our forefathers never dreamed of—things that people in some parts of the world still don't have. Think of luxuries like . . .

- Drive-through restaurants
- Microwave ovens
- Television
- Air conditioning
- Jet travel
- Fax machines
- Video cameras
- *Cliff's Notes*
- Acne medicine
- Cars
- Telephones
- Indoor plumbing
- Computers
- Washing machines
- Medical technology
- Other: _____

There's something else we Christians often take for granted—our access to God, the privilege of coming into His presence anytime we want. Too often the thrill of being in His presence has long since faded. We forget that it hasn't always been possible to get this close to God, particularly in regard to prayer. Simply put, the presence of God hasn't always been something every believer could experience in the same way we do now.

1. Looking back in the Old Testament, how did God used to make His presence known? (See Exodus 13:21, 22.)

2. How did God's people respond to His presence? (See Exodus 20:18, 19.)

Under the Old Testament law system, God seemed distant to the average Jew. The typical Israelite could pray to God, but could not approach Him physically. There were special laws God made concerning how He was to be approached. The Book of Leviticus records God's laws governing how to come into His presence.

While God was still the Israelites' God, getting in to see Him was not even considered an option for the average believer—that is, until Christ came.

3. Explain how Jesus replaced this system of approaching God. (See Hebrews 9:11-15.)

4. What happened at the exact moment Christ died? (See Matthew 27:51.)

5. Based on what you know about the holy of holies, what do you think is the significance of Christ's death?

3 The Ultimate Backstage Pass

A teenage guy was trying to sneak his date back into her home because it was very late. To their surprise, they were met at the top of the stairs by the girl's very angry father. He bellowed, "Young man, didn't I hear the clock strike four when you just walked in the door with my daughter?" The clever boy replied, "Yes sir, you did. It was going to strike eleven, but I grabbed it and

held the gong so that it wouldn't wake you up." The father mumbled to himself, "Doggone it! Why didn't I think of that excuse in my day?"

Some people are good at coming up with great excuses for all kinds of situations—lost homework, being late for work, missing the big youth event at church, late payments, etc. But what good excuse do you and I have for not spending time in the presence of God? Do we realize what an awesome privilege it is for us to come before Him? Some of us wouldn't think of turning down backstage passes to our favorite band's concert, and yet we often turn down opportunities to go into the very throne room of God Almighty! What's wrong with this picture?

To help us fully appreciate this private audience we have with the Lord, let's reexamine the reasons why our access to God is such a privilege.

1. Read Hebrews 4:14-16. What is there about Jesus that should draw you to God's throne?

2. What should be our attitude in approaching God? Why?

3. What does God say we will always receive? (See also Romans 5:1, 2.)

4. Describe another ministry Jesus provides for you in God's presence. (See Hebrews 7:24, 25; 9:24 and Romans 8:34.)

5. Looking at Hebrews 10:19-22, what might be the greatest personal advantage you gain from being in God's presence?

6. What is God's promise to you when you enter His presence? (See James 4:8.)

When you're experiencing tough times, nothing is more comforting than having a friend who sticks by your side through it all. In Jesus, you have a friend who promises to do that and more. He will never leave your side (Hebrews 13:5). You can always count on Him to be there for you. Your access to God and His nearness to you are available twenty-four hours a day, seven days a week, three hundred and sixty five days a year (three hundred and sixty six during Leap Years).

God is there . . .

- when you feel far away from Him.
- when you have been betrayed or disappointed by a friend.
- when you have sinned.
- when your family is falling apart.
- when your day has been a disaster.
- when you feel like a failure.
- when you're in physical pain.
- when you're facing a huge problem.
- when you're under attack.
- when your future seems uncertain.
- when you have to say goodbye to old friends.
- when your strength to carry on is gone.
- when you're alone.
- when your burden is too big to bear.

He is there.

Deep in the Arabian Desert stands a small fortress. Thomas Edward Lawrence, better know as "Lawrence of Arabia," often used it. Though not very impressive to look at, the little fort was a secure refuge. Its primary strength was its security. When under attack, Lawrence knew that he could retreat there. It was during those times that all of the resources of the fortress became his. The food and water stored there would sustain him. The strength and safety of the fortress would protect him. Its strength became his strength. The great Lawrence of Arabia trusted and depended on the old fort, and it kept him safe and secure from many outside threats and dangers.

When through prayer you enter God's presence, you'll find a fortress of security and protection. You'll discover it to be sufficient for all of your needs. You'll also find that you can be at peace there. Drawing near to God, you can be free from worry and can rest from the stresses and problems of everyday life. So why not make it a practice—a habit, a way of life—to run to that fortress often?

God is not like a political figure, a celebrity, or some business executive who has scores of secretaries and security personnel that you have to go through to get to Him. His door is always open. You are always welcome in His presence. He is never too busy for you. Remember, you are His beloved child. So be open and honest with Him. Offer Him your burdens as well as your life in a fresh way each time you come before Him. And remember, there's no appointment necessary.

PRAY About It

What's going on in your life right now? What are you facing that you need to bring before the Lord? Practice your privilege right now by coming with confidence into God's presence, bringing your concerns. Pour out your heart to Him in prayer. Thank Him for inviting you into His "holy of holies," and most of all, enjoy being in His company.

WEEK 9 An In-the-Body Experience

Your Identification with the Body of Christ

My Identity: I am identified with God's people.

1 Dance Fever

Life is full of embarrassing moments. We've all experienced them. Times we wished we could just vaporize into thin air. Memories we wish we could erase. Events that at the time seemed bigger than life itself. One of mine (and I've had many) came in the seventh grade. The event was my first dance. You know, guys and girls. I had been looking forward to it for weeks. It would be my first opportunity to slow dance with my girlfriend. That afternoon, I had patiently supervised while my mom ironed my clothes. I meticulously combed my hair, making sure that not a strand was out of place. I strategically applied my dad's cologne for added effect. I was dressed to kill and prepared for anything.

Well, almost anything. When I walked into the room, I discovered to my horror that I was the only one wearing penny loafers. All I could see was a room full of tennis shoes. It seemed as if every eye in the place was glued to my feet. I felt like my shoes were flashing neon signs. I immediately realized I had made a big mistake. I had committed a major social no-no. An unforgivable blunder. This was definitely not going to be a "Kodak moment." I had worn the wrong thing. I officially didn't belong. I feared this moment would mark me for the rest of the year. I would be branded as a nerd. I would become "Loafer Boy" to my class. So in a panic, I made a dash for the back of the room and dove under the punch table, where I successfully hid for the next thirty minutes. Fortunately, however, my friends understood my dilemma and were able to coax me out. Later, I did get to dance with my date. By that time, to my relief, most people were dancing in their socks.

I never wore those shoes again.

What was your most embarrassing junior high moment? (C'mon, be honest.)

One of the greatest desires you and I have is the desire to *belong* to something. To have an identity. To be a part of a group. To be a member of something. To be associated with a group. To be accepted. To be included—like me at the dance. That's why people want to identify themselves so strongly with certain groups like fraternities, sororities, skaters, dopers, athletes, musicians, cowboys, intellectuals, socialites, hippies, activists, and even street gangs. Most people would rather die than not have an identity. The desire to belong is so strong that we will go to just about any lengths to fulfill it. In short, every nobody wants to be a somebody.

Looking at the previous list, name the three most popular groups at your school.

1. _____

2. _____

3. _____

With which one would you most identify? Why?

2 Membership Has Its Privileges

The Bible says you are a member of a unique and special group called the *church*. The church is not a building or an organization or a club. It's people. And the great thing about being a member is that you don't have to be pretty or handsome, rich or talented, athletic or academic. You don't even have to be like everybody else in the group. You can be an individual—the person God made you to be. The only qualification for membership is that you know Jesus Christ as your Lord and Savior.

When you think of the church, think of two kinds:

1. The *universal* church, which includes all believers around the world

2. The *local* church, the people you worship with on Sunday

The universal church is made up of all Christians, while the local church may have some non-Christians who attend. In fact, you *want* your church to have non-Christians coming!

In this chapter, you'll understand your membership in the church more clearly in light of three relationships:

• A new relationship with Christ

• A new relationship with Christians

• A new relationship with the world

Let's start by looking at your new relationship with Christ. At salvation, you are united with Christ as a part of His body, the church. Because of this, you have a new kind of relationship with Jesus Christ.

1. How does the Bible picture this relationship?

Colossians 1:18

- Jesus is the _____ ; I am His _____ .

Ephesians 2:19

- Jesus is the _____ ; I am a _____ of God's household.

Ephesians 5:25-27

- Jesus is the _____ ; I am His _____ .

John 15:5

- Jesus is the _____ ; I am the _____ .

2. Is there a common theme running through these word pictures? If so, what is it?

3. What are the benefits of being related to Christ in each of these ways?

3 In Desperate Need of a Clue

A physician recommended to one of his patients that he lose about forty pounds. The doctor's instructions were that the patient run five miles a day for the next 100 days. The overweight patient called the doctor exactly 100 days later and complained that he was unhappy with the weight-loss program.

"But haven't you lost the weight?" asked the physician.

"Sure I did," the patient replied. "But now I'm 500 miles from home!"

This guy is officially "clueless." He's like the person who thinks a thesaurus is a kind of dinosaur or who thinks a megabyte is something you take out of a Big Mac! But some Christians are like this man in their approach to church—clueless. They don't really know why they go to church from week to week. They're just going through the motions. They're just there. They get into a rut that soon becomes a meaningless routine. They lose sight of the purpose of being a part of a local body of believers. Their Christianity has deteriorated into "Churchianity."

But there is a purpose for being in the local church. In fact, there are several very strong reasons that you should commit yourself to a local body of believers. There are things the church can do for you as well as things you can do for others in the church. These things, when put together, help answer the question "How do I get the most out of church?"

This section will help you maximize your relationships with others in the church. These are the things that can make church come alive to you.

1. Look up Ephesians 4:11-13. Write down the reasons God placed you in His body, the church.

If you desire for those things to be true in your life, then allow yourself to be taught God's Word regularly in church.

2. What about your relationships with other believers? What can you do for them?

- I Corinthians 12:4-7

- I Corinthians 12:14-21

Summarize the previous two passages in one sentence.

3. Looking at I Corinthians 12:26, in what kinds of situations could you see yourself practicing this truth?

4. Read I John 4:21 and Hebrews 10:24, 25. What three commands does God give in these verses?

5. What does the author add in Hebrews 10:25 to further motivate us?

6. Write down one thing you will do this week to encourage someone in your church (a pastor, youth leader, teacher, friend).

Can you see how these things might prevent church from becoming boring to you? It's hard to be bored when you're being challenged in your walk with God through the teaching of His Word and when you're busy meeting other's needs. That's part of what it means to be identified with the body of Christ. But there's a third aspect of being a member of His body.

4 Keeping Water Outta Your Boat

As believers, we not only have a new relationship with Christ and with other Christians, but we also have a new and different relationship to the world. We have been "called out" of the world and are no longer controlled by its secular thinking. What should our relationship to the world be like now that we are identified with the body of Christ? Take a look at what God says.

1. Read II Corinthians 6:14-17 out loud. What do these verses say you have in common with unbelievers and the world?

2. That sounds kind of harsh. What do you think Paul means when he says these things?

3. How does Jesus shed light on this truth in John 17:14, 15?

Concerning our relationship to the world, Bible teacher John MacArthur has said, "You have to keep your boat in the water without getting the water in your boat."

4. In what sense should Christians love the world (John 3:16)?

5. How did Jesus say the world would treat His church? (See John 15:18, 19 and I John 3:13.)

6. Read Matthew 16:18. Describe the church's ultimate effect on the world and evil forces.

7. Summarize in your own words what your relationship with the world is to be like.

KEEP In Mind

Your physical body needs a head to survive. The head gives direction and authority. The individual parts of the body need one another. They naturally serve one another (like when one part is hurt, the rest of the body rushes to bring help and healing). But your body also must protect itself from danger and infection in order to stay healthy. God's church is no different. Each of us is to submit his or her life to the head, Jesus Christ. We must receive God's instruction and serve one another. And we must live in the world and seek to love people without becoming a part of its way of thinking. But also keep in mind that we are joined together as the body of Christ. You see, our desire to belong is met in the church. We are a part of the most important group of people in the world! We are somebody. You are somebody. And the more we identify ourselves with God's church, the more we will have a true "in the body" experience.

Make three concrete applications of your identification with the body of Christ.

1. I will submit myself to Christ this week by . . .

2. I will encourage someone in my church this week by . . .

3. I will keep myself from being identified in some wrong way with the world by . . .

PRAY About It

Spend time now praying for your church, its pastors and leaders, your brothers and sisters in Christ. Find out from them how you can pray for them specifically in the weeks and months ahead. Make a decision to regularly pray for their needs.

My Assurance Policy

Your Assurance of Salvation

My Identity: I am confident in God's gift of salvation.

1 Get a Grip

On a commuter flight from Portland, Maine, to Boston, pilot Henry Dempsey heard a strange noise coming from the rear of the plane. Concerned, he turned the controls over to the copilot and went back to check it out. As he reached the tail section, the jet hit an air pocket and he was thrown out the rear door. The copilot saw the red light that indicated an open door, and immediately radioed the nearest airport requesting an emergency landing. He reported that the pilot had fallen out of the plane, and asked that a helicopter be dispatched to search that area of the ocean.

But the search didn't last long. Airport officials spotted Henry Dempsey—holding on to the outdoor ladder of the aircraft! Somehow, as he was being sucked out of the plane, he had managed to catch the ladder and hold on for ten minutes as the plane flew 200 miles per hour at an altitude of 4,000 feet. Then, while the jet was landing, he somehow kept his head from hitting the runway, which was a mere twelve inches away. Not surprisingly, it took airport personnel several minutes to pry Dempsey's fingers from the ladder.

A question many sincere students often ask is "How can I know I'm a Christian?" People expected Henry Dempsey to be lost. Despite tremendous opposition, he was not lost.

Do you think it's normal to doubt your salvation? Why or why not?

What are some reasons that Christians question whether or not they are genuinely converted?

2 The Anchor of Hope

Consider the following two common case scenarios:

Case 1

Mark is depressed. He *thinks* he became a Christian at age four, but because he was so young, he's not sure if he really understood what he was doing. After all, children will do anything to please their parents. Since that time, Mark's Christian life has been an up-and-down experience. And that makes him wonder if he truly is a Christian.

Case 2

Jenny became a Christian at youth camp last summer. She came out of a sinful past, having done drugs and slept with her boyfriend. Over the past year, she's seen a dramatic change in her life. But last week, she went to a friend's birthday party to which someone brought beer. Though Jenny reasoned that just one beer couldn't hurt, she ended up getting drunk and saying and doing some things that now she's very embarrassed about. She wonders if a real Christian could ever sin like that. She's definitely living in "Doubt City."

What hope can we offer Mark and Jenny?

The good news is that the hope you and I have concerns the Bible's assurance of our salvation.

I John 5:13
I write these things to you who believe in the name of the Son of God
so that you may know that you have eternal life.

1. What would you say is the key encouraging word for doubting Christians in this verse?

2. Look at Colossians 1:5, 27. What is the difference between the way many people use the word "hope" and the way the Bible uses it?

3. Here are five thoughts to help you deal with doubts about your salvation.

• Salvation is by _____ through _____ (Ephesians 2:8, 9).

Do you have faith in a gracious God?

• Saving faith is followed by _____ (James 2:17).

This kind of faith is in contrast to mere intellectual faith (2:19) and dead faith (2:26). Both of these would lead to a false assurance of salvation.

• God the Father has _____ your sins (Isaiah 43:25).

That's a pretty amazing case of amnesia for Someone who knows everything!

• God the Son has _____ all of your sins to the cross (Colossians 2:13, 14).

Excuse me? How many?

• God the Spirit _____ with your spirit that you are God's child (Romans 8:16).

The Spirit was also given to you as God's solemn pledge that He will see you through all the way to heaven (Ephesians 1:13, 14).

3 Your Faith Assurance Policy

Have you ever met a person who seemed almost scared to death of other people? Perhaps the person was really likable, but lacked a strong sense of self-esteem and, therefore, lacked assurance about himself or herself. Singer Karen Carpenter (who died from the effects of anorexia) "had it made" in the eyes of millions of people; yet inside her own head, she was all wrong. She badly needed her confidence strengthened.

What happens at the psychological level also happens at the spiritual level. Some Christians doubt their own value before God. They need restored assurance. What ideas in the Bible can bolster a doubting Christian's confidence?

• First, believing what the Bible actually says about Christians, rather than trusting the way we're feeling at a particular moment, is one way of assuring ourselves.

1. What does Ephesians 1:7 say about Christians?

2. How is Ephesians 2:1-6 assuring?

3. What have we got going for us according to Romans 8:31-34?

• If a house plant seems to be drooping or wilting, what can you do? (Revive it; cultivate it; give it water.) By the same token, what resources or aids can help you cultivate confidence in your relationship with Christ, according to Jude 20 and 21?

• Christians are children of God. God is our heavenly Father. How many parents have you known who kicked their children out of the family? (Hopefully, none.) God is a perfect Parent (who may chasten us—see Hebrews 12:7-11). All that God does for us He does out of love. Have you memorized any verses that tell us how loving God is toward us or how trustworthy He is? (Check out I John 3:1-3 or I John 3:19, 20.)

• We all blow it at times. Remember Abraham (who lied about his wife), Moses (who killed a man), David (who was guilty of adultery and a murder conspiracy), and Peter (who denied that he knew Christ)? Did God turn His back on any of these Bible characters? No! Absolutely not!

Assurance is a lot like the person who comes to a frozen pond in winter. He is afraid to venture firmly out onto the ice. Then, while shaking, he hears sleigh bells coming from behind. A sleigh team plunges right out onto the ice and crosses the river. All of a sudden, the first person feels great assurance. Why? He now sees that what was underneath him all along was able to hold him perfectly (Jude 24, 25).

KEEP In Mind

God is not some cruel tyrant who wants you to live in perpetual fear. He doesn't want you to live in doubt, but rather in confident assurance. Christ's death was sufficient payment for all of your sin. The key that unlocks the door to your assurance of salvation is your trust in what God says in His Word. The stronger you trust in the truth of the Word, the weaker your doubts will become. Declare war on your doubt with God's Word. Fight the good fight of faith.

PRAY About It

List any doubts you may have had about your salvation and pray through some of the Scripture passages given in this chapter. Thank God that He has given you a way to remove your doubts. And if you have been doubting, destroy those doubts right now in prayer by praying God's truth back to Him.

How Do I Respond?

Congratulations! You've just finished studying what most young people are afraid to touch—theology. Many people think theology is dull and dry, but you've seen a much more colorful side of the subject. You've seen how each truth makes a difference in your life. Now you come to an even greater "So What?" section of this book.

In this section, you're no longer dealing with your position in Christ or your perspective on your relationship with Him. It's time to go deeper into application and put into practice what you've discovered.

Think of these last five chapters as a "how to" manual for your Christian life. In them you'll learn how to stay on the road to spiritual maturity, how to handle the "sticky issues" of the Christian life, how to become more like Jesus, how to bounce back when you fall into sin, and how to anticipate and prepare for the ultimate graduation ceremony God has planned for you.

When you're done, you will have grown closer to and more in love with your great God and Savior. You'll know how to apply the *Done Deal* to the daily grind!

WEEK 11 Moving toward Maturity

Growing Stronger in Christ

My Ability in Christ: I can grow.

1 Oh, Baby!

He was born on February 22, 1918, weighing a modest 8 ½ pounds. But following an operation at age two, his growth began to accelerate. By age five he was already 5'4" tall. At ten he was 6'5" tall. And by the time he was 22 years old, Robert Wadlow stood a record 8 feet, 11 inches tall and weighed 430 pounds! He also wore a 37AA shoe size. Can you imagine playing basketball against this guy?!

What are some things you would do if you were that tall?

2 Growing Beyond Goo-Goo

Why are people naturally attracted to babies? Babies seem to have an innocent charm that causes others to give them love and attention. However, babies don't stay small and cuddly. They soon grow, leaving their cuteness and "baby fat" behind. Through the awkward preteen and junior high years, they finally become fully grown, physically mature.

But suppose you saw someone your age walking across campus in a big diaper, sucking on a bottle. Assuming it wasn't a costume or a fraternity initiation, but real, what would you be thinking? Imagine this person, who had never grown out of diapers or had never been weaned from a bottle.

As bizarre as this sounds, if God were to let us peek into the spiritual world, we might see the same thing happening spiritually in people's lives. Why do many Christians seem to be weak, undiscerning, and immature? Why don't they understand more about God and the Christian life? Why are they still dealing with "infant issues" in the Christian life? The answer lies in their spiritual growth—or lack of it.

1. What is God's desire for us as His children? (See II Peter 3:18.)

2. Why do you think growth is so crucial for a baby? What similarities are there between physical and spiritual growth?

3. Why is it that some people fail to grow physically?

4. According to Matthew 13:20-22, what are some reasons why growth never takes place in some professing Christians?

5. How does Hebrews 5:11-14 describe Christians who fail to grow?

6. What is the goal of our growth? (See Colossians 1:28 and Hebrews 6:1.)

If you fail to grow physically, that means something is wrong with you physically. If you fail to grow spiritually, that means something isn't right spiritually. Growth is normal and natural. Not growing is abnormal. Like plants and trees, we need to grow. We need deep roots and lots of "watering" if we are to grow into spiritual maturity, which is God's will for us all (Colossians 1:28). But how does that become a reality in our lives?

3 It's the Law, Ma'am

Nearly every state has laws on its books which, when written, made perfect sense, but now are clearly obsolete. Here are some of the more interesting, obscure laws on the books throughout the country.

- To take a bath in Boston, you must have a doctor's written prescription.
- A Louisiana law says you can grow as tall as you like.
- In the Pine Island District of Minnesota, a man must tip his hat when passing a cow.
- It is against the law in North Carolina to sing out of tune.
- You are not permitted to swim on dry land in Santa Ana, California.

- In Idaho, you cannot fish for trout from the back of a giraffe.
- A law in Pocatello, Idaho, makes it illegal to look gloomy.
- It is unlawful to lasso a fish in Knoxville, Tennessee.

These laws are not only silly, but ridiculous! But when it comes to our growth in Christ, the spiritual laws in God's Book make perfect sense to us.
We could define spiritual growth as the process by which our position in Christ slowly becomes the practice of our lives. Our position (see chapters 1-10 in this book) never changes. However, our practice (growth) does. If growth is so important, and if growing means that we get to experience more of what we have learned so far, then what are some principles concerning our spiritual growth? Let's look at some laws of spiritual development.

1. Spiritual growth is more than intellectual _____ (I Corinthians 8:1).

Jesus' sharpest condemnation was to the religious leaders of His day who knew lots of Bible verses, but never knew the Lord.

2. Growth is more than performing religious _____ (Matthew 7:21-23).

By contrast, spiritual growth is just that—spiritual. What does this spiritual growth require?

3. Read Philippians 3:12. What does Paul say here about his spiritual maturity?

This statement takes on added meaning when you realize that Paul had been growing in Christ for some thirty years! So *time* would be a key element in our spiritual growth. Remember, when God wants to make a mighty oak, He takes one hundred years. When He wants to make a squash, He takes two months. But time alone cannot produce a mature Christian (see Hebrews 5:12).

4. What would be another factor in our growth? (See I Peter 2:2.)

5. What do you know about a baby's desire for milk? How should that compare to our "craving" and hunger for God's Word?

6. What is another important element in our growth? (See Romans 1:17.)

7. In what way would this contribute to your spiritual growth?

8. What would be the ultimate factor in your growth? (See I Corinthians 3:6.)

9. What does maturity begin to look like as you grow in Christ? How can you be sure that you are growing?

4 Modern Maturity

World famous prizefighter Muhammad Ali was once asked by a young man what he should do with his life. The heavyweight's reply was "Stay in college, get the knowledge. And stay there until you're through. If they can make penicillin out of moldy bread, they can sure make something out of you."

In case you tend to get discouraged about your growth, remember that God is making something out of you. And He promises to never give up on you until He's done (Philippians 1:6). But wouldn't it be great to actually be able to measure your spiritual growth? When you were little, maybe your mom or dad put little marks on the wall to measure your growth from month to month. That way you could see how far and fast you were growing and maturing physically. Are there similar "growth marks" to measure our spiritual maturity? How can we chart our internal spiritual development without becoming legalistic?

The Bible is filled with signs of growth we can look for in our lives. With these "marks of maturity," we can get an idea of what's going on in our relationship with Christ. Though they're not all-inclusive, look up the following verses and jot down some of the signs of spiritual growth you can be looking for.

• Hebrews 5:14

A maturing Christian . . .

• Ephesians 4:13

A maturing Christian . . .

• I John 3:24

A maturing Christian . . .

• I John 5:20, 21

A maturing Christian . . .

- II Timothy 2:15b

A maturing Christian . . .

- I John 4:16-18

A maturing Christian . . .

I once had a friend whose life dream was to be a professional basketball player. There was only one problem—he wasn't tall enough. So his number one desire was to grow physically taller, and he was willing to do almost anything to achieve this goal. He took vitamins, received hormone injections, and did special exercises. In fact, so great was his desire to grow that he actually went to an out-of-state clinic and had himself "stretched"! And though he never made it to the NBA, his desire for growth and greatness was unmatched.

KEEP In Mind

How badly do you want to grow in your relationship with Christ? How great is your desire to become strong in your faith and mature as a Christian? What are you willing to do to accomplish your desire? Are you presently growing? If not, will you ask God to help you begin changing that today? Keep in mind that growth takes time. There is no instant growth, no overnight spirituality, no "drive-through" disciples. You can't microwave yourself into maturity. Instead, you must desire to grow and "eat" regularly. Learn to feed yourself. Focus on developing your walk with Christ and watch for the marks of maturity to show up in your daily life. That way, you'll head down the road beyond diapers and bottles.

PRAY About It

Spend some time praying specifically for the desire to grow and for the marks of maturity to be shown in your life over time.

WEEK ◀12 Give Me Liberty?

Balancing Your Freedom in Christ

My Ability in Christ: I can be discerning.

1 Gray Matters

Question:

What do the following things have in common?

Drinking
Wearing makeup
Going to R-rated movies
Going to PG movies
Renting movies
Working on Sunday
Wearing jeans to church
Listening to rock music
Listening to Christian rock music
Electric guitars and drums
Wearing expensive clothes
Guys with long hair
Girls with short hair
Guys with shaved heads
Kissing on the first date

Kissing on any date
Kissing
Car dating
Dating
Dancing
Going to a secular rock concert
Staying out past midnight
Reading romance novels
Joining a fraternity or sorority
Attending a party where alcohol is served
Eating at a restaurant that serves alcohol
Mixed swimming
Having church services twice on Sunday
Christian girls wearing bikinis

Answer:

These are mostly modern problems that are not specifically commented upon in Scripture. They can be controversial and can produce disagreement between Christians, since some of the issues are considered to be clearly sinful while others are thought of as perfectly legitimate. There are an endless number of these gray areas, depending on a person's church or family background, his or her understanding of Scripture, and his or her personal experience.

Write down some additional issues in your home, church, or community that would qualify as "gray areas."

Choose one of these issues, either in your list or the one provided earlier. Jot it down. We'll come back to it later.

2 Don't!

Josh is the star quarterback of his high school football team. One Thursday afternoon, he and some fellow teammates decided to go see the movie *Rudy*, which is about a young man's dream to play football for the legendary Fighting Irish of Notre Dame. After the movie, Josh and his buddies were high-fiving each other, inspired to play their crosstown rivals the following evening. But as they left the theater, they were confronted by a group of ministry students from a nearby college. These students told Josh and his friends that they were going to hell because they had watched a movie that contained foul language. But instead of arguing with them, Josh and his friends just went home.

What do you think?
• Was Josh wrong to see the movie?
• Were the college students right?
• Should Josh have told the ministry students that *they* were the ones going to hell?

• Did Josh do the right thing by walking away?
• Would you say this is a clear issue of right and wrong? Or does this qualify as a gray area?

When discerning whether or not to participate in certain activities, there are two dangerous traps to avoid. One is the trap of falling into legalism, and the other is the danger of abusing your liberty in Christ. Let's look first at the trap of legalism.

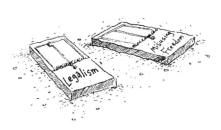

1. How would you define "legalism"?
    a. Taking human's rules and making them God's rules
    b. Trying to keep the Old Testament law
    c. Thinking that adherence to the "rules" of the Bible is what saves you
    d. Believing that certain religious behavior makes you acceptable to God
    e. All of the above

2. Why do you think being legalistic is so dangerous?

Colossians 2:22
These are all destined to perish with use, because they are based on human commands and teachings.

3. What does legalism lead to? (See Galatians 5:1, 2.)

4. Why is legalism powerless to change us?
    • Colossians 2:20-23

• Romans 8:3

5. Can you think of any group in the New Testament that would qualify as "legalists"?

6. According to Matthew 23:13-15, why was Jesus' condemnation to them so harsh?

When you approach gray areas, keep in mind that rules for rules' sake is legalism. That only leads to spiritual slavery again, which can never change you or please God or improve your standing before Him. Legalism is not spirituality.

3 The Responsibility of Freedom

Legalism is not the only trap we should avoid. There is another equally dangerous extreme we should also steer clear of. It's the trap of misusing and abusing our freedom in Christ. In the strictest sense, there is no real freedom without responsibility. Take your driver's license, for example. With it, you have the freedom to drive on any highway, street, and backroad in the country. But you also have the responsibility to obey the traffic laws. Abusing that freedom might involve driving recklessly, breaking the speed limit, or carving a new road through your school principal's front yard. In that case, freedom might also involve a hefty fine!

So how are we to use our freedom in Christ when it comes to those gray areas of life?

Galatians 5:13
You, my brothers, were called to be free. But do not use your freedom to indulge the sinful nature; rather, serve one another in love.

1. What perspective on our freedom in Christ can you gain from this verse?

A good question to ask yourself might be "Is this activity appealing to my sinful nature?"

2. How could God use this kind of lifestyle as a witness to others? (See I Peter 2:11, 12.)

Think of your liberty in Christ not as the freedom to do what you want to do, but rather the freedom to do what you ought to do.

3. Read I Corinthians 8:1-13. What does this passage say about exercising your freedom in the gray areas?

4. Summarize the key principle in one sentence.

Imagine that you are approached one day by an older church member who claims that your music (or car, hair, etc.) is offensive to him. When asked why, he explains that your music identifies you with the evil in the world and not with Christ. Would this principle of causing others to stumble apply here? If not, why?

5. Can you think of a freedom you would voluntarily give up for the sake of another Christian?

Now take the issue you chose at the beginning of this session and answer the following questions.

• Do I believe that this activity is inherently sinful?

• Am I avoiding this activity in order to feel "spiritual" about myself?

• Do I equate participating in (or not participating in) this activity with being pleasing to God?

• Will my being involved with this cause me to indulge my flesh?

• Will it cause a brother or sister to stumble into sin?

• Am I willing to do without it for the sake of another?

How can you be sure that an issue is not a gray area, but an area that should be avoided?

1. When it is forbidden by parents (Ephesians 6:1-3) or church leaders (Hebrews 13:7-17)

2. When the Bible states that it is a sin (Romans 14:23)

3. When it causes you to think impure thoughts (Philippians 4:8)

4. When it causes others to sin (I Corinthians 8:1-13)

5. When it hinders the effectiveness of the Gospel (I Corinthians 9:19-23)

KEEP In Mind

We all need the wisdom that comes from God's Word and godly people to keep us balanced in our lives. The key word here is "balanced." We have to avoid both extremes of legalism and license—needless rules and excess liberty. True spirituality is inward and not measured by human rules. To avoid all contact with anything that could be considered a gray area hinders the Great Commission. By the same token, wisdom says to think before you act, making sure that you are living responsibly under God's grace.

PRAY About It

Ask God to give you wisdom as you face gray areas in your life. Pray to be balanced, avoiding both legalism and license.

WEEK ◀13 Family Resemblances

Becoming Like Christ

My Ability in Christ: I can become like Christ.

1 A Masterpiece in the Making

If you've ever played the piano, you probably know what a Steinway is. These skillfully crafted pianos are some of the world's finest. They are built today exactly as they were almost 150 years ago when Henry Steinway first began crafting them. Today, some 200 skilled artisans and craftsmen combine their talents to produce the 12,000 parts that go into a Steinway. One crucial part in the process is the "rim-bending," in which 18 layers of bonded maple 22 feet long are bent around an iron press. This creates the shape of a grand piano. Add to this five coats of superior lacquer for an outer glow. After the strings are added, the piano is finally taken to the Pounder Room where all of its keys are mercilessly tested 10,000 times to ensure flawless responsiveness. When the process is finished, the piano can proudly bear the name Steinway.

As Christians, we are like one of those Steinway masterpieces, "handcrafted" by God into the image of His Son Jesus Christ. As we follow Him, we begin taking on His character and attributes. This chapter is all about helping you pursue the image of Christ in your day-to-day life.

Before you get into the chapter, write down the name of someone you really admire. Include two or three of his or her characteristics that cause you to look up to that person.

2 Born to Conform

The next time you're at a friend's house, take a look around to see if you notice any family resemblances or dominant traits. Your friend may have his or her father's eyes, or his or her mom's nose. Perhaps there may be a likeness in hair color, skin tone, or facial qualities. As a follower of Christ, you want people to recognize you because of your resemblance to the Lord. And in this process of growing into His likeness, both you and God have an active part. You don't "let go and let God," but neither can you do it by yourself. Rather, it's a joint venture, a team effort. You are "partners" with God, so to speak.

1. What does God say His commitment to you is? (See Romans 8:29.)

II Corinthians 3:18
And we, who with unveiled faces all reflect the Lord's glory, are being transformed into his
likeness with ever-increasing glory, which comes from the Lord, who is the Spirit.

2. What verb tense is used in this verse? What do you think that signifies? (See also Philippians 1:6.)

3. For how long is God committed to this process?

4. OK, that's God's part. Now what's your role in becoming like Christ? What are some things you can do that will help mold your inner character into Christlikeness? (See Romans 12:1, 2.)

5. There are both positive and negative commands in Romans 12:1, 2. What are they?

- Positive commands—

- Negative commands—

6. Read Colossians 3:1, 2. These verses sound "spiritual," but what do you think they mean practically?

7. After looking at Philippians 3:17 and I Corinthians 11:1, how would you go about finding ways to live out these verses?

The Ultimate Example

What are some of Jesus' character traits that you could emulate?

Jesus is the perfect example to us . . .

- in His service to others (John 13:12-15)
- in His suffering (I Peter 2:21-23)
- in His perseverance (Hebrews 12:2, 3)
- in His devotion to the Father (Mark 1:35)
- in His love and compassion (Mark 1:40, 41)
- in His zeal for God (Matthew 21:12, 13)
- in His forgiveness of His enemies (Luke 23:34)
- in His humility (Philippians 2:8)
- in His obedience to the Father (John 4:34; 9:4)
- in His victory over temptation (Matthew 4:1-11)

3 The Road to Character

British author C. S. Lewis wrote, "God whispers to us in our pleasures, speaks in our conscience, and shouts in our pain." Though God uses many different people and things to conform us into the likeness of His Son, perhaps none is more common and (at times) more painful than trials. When we go through hard times, our faith and character are tested unlike at any other time. What is it about dealing with difficult circumstances that can cause us to become more like Christ?

Romans 5:3-5
Not only so, but we also rejoice in our sufferings, because we know that suffering produces perseverance; perseverance, character; and character, hope. And hope does not disappoint us, because God has poured out His love into our hearts by the Holy Spirit, whom he has given us.

1. Why do you suppose Paul chose the phrase *"in* our sufferings" and not *"because of* our sufferings"? What's the difference?

2. Rewrite Romans 5:3-5, charting their cause-effect relationship.

Suffering produces _____ .

_____ produces _____ .

_____ produces _____ .

_____ doesn't _____ .

In short, suffering produces character.

3. In light of the theme of this chapter, what might the "hope" refer to here?

4. What word in this passage tells you that this hope is not just a wish, but a guarantee?

5. Are you facing a tough time right now? If not, you may soon.

Maybe your struggle involves you and your . . .

- family
- friends
- job
- girlfriend/boyfriend
- schoolwork
- health
- athletics
- church
- parents
- other: _____

How does God expect you to know what character lesson to learn through this trial? How does He promise to help you? (See James 1:5.)

Imagine this: You can actually face your problems and have pure joy in spite of them because God promises to use those trials to transform you into Christlikeness! But the key to doing this is looking to God the whole time and depending on Him to get you through. That way His wisdom becomes yours—His strength is your strength.

KEEP In Mind

Years ago, there was a girl who was the daughter of a royal family in Europe. The only problem was that she had a big, unsightly nose that, in her eyes, destroyed her beauty and made her an ugly person. Finally her family hired the best plastic surgeon to change the contour of the girl's nose. After surgery, there came the moment when the bandages were removed and the doctor saw that the operation had been a total success. All of the ugly contours were gone. Her nose was different. When the incisions and redness disappeared, she would be the beautiful girl she had dreamed of being for years. The doctor held up a mirror for the girl to see, but so deeply embedded was her image of her old face that, upon looking into the mirror, she burst into tears and cried, "I knew it wouldn't work!" Months passed until the girl could finally look at herself in the mirror to see the change that had taken place.

So it is with you. God is using trials and your devotion to Him to slowly change you into Christlikeness. Think of it—His character can be yours! Could there be any more attractive likeness to pursue than His? Focus on being like Jesus, and watch God, like a skilled surgeon, transform you into the character image of His Son.

PRAY About It

What are you facing these days? Ask God in prayer for wisdom to know how to deal with those trials, and faith to trust in His power as you endure them.

WEEK 14 After a Fall

Experiencing God's Forgiveness

My Ability in Christ: I can overcome failure.

1 Strike Three!

Sometimes you can feel like such a failure.

- You fought with your parents.
- You gave in to that same habit . . . again.
- You fumbled ethically, made a moral error, struck out spiritually.

You sinned.

Let's be brutally honest. We all struggle with sin, don't we? Temptations, old habits, sins we thought we had conquered, doubts, bad decisions, bruised relationships, broken promises, lust, sex, pride, judging others, hypocrisy, rebellion—the list goes on and on.

The next time you're feeling like a total failure, consider some people whose shortcomings have been made public knowledge over the years.

• Growing up in England, he spoke with a lisp. He was never a scholar in school. When war broke out, the military rejected him because they needed "real men." He once rose to address the House of Commons, and they all walked out on him. Refusing to let failure get the best of him, he kept on going until one day he became Prime Minister of Great Britain, leading his country to victory in a world war. That young man was Sir Winston Churchill, whose iron will to persevere turned a lisping boy into one of this century's greatest orators.

• He failed in business in '31, was defeated for the legislature in '32, again failed in business in '33, was defeated for elector in '40, defeated for Congress in '43, defeated again in '48, defeated for Senate in '55, defeated for the vice presidential nomination in '56, and defeated for the Senate again in '58. But Abraham Lincoln did not let failure defeat him.

• Babe Ruth struck out 1,330 times, almost doubling the number of home runs he hit.

But we're not talking about baseball or politics here. This is real life. More importantly, we're talking about our relationship with God. Sin is serious business. When you sin, usually you feel guilty. But what does that guilt also cause you personally to feel? Put a check beside the following choices that apply to you.

___ Sadness
___ Depression
___ Hopelessness
___ Fear
___ Bitterness
___ Separation
___ Desire for cleansing
___ Despair
___ Anger
___ Weakness
___ Denial
___ As if God is angry at you

2 Finding Forgiveness

Many years ago, Sir Arthur Conan Doyle decided to play a practical joke on twelve of his friends. He sent them each a telegram that simply read, "Flee at once . . . all is discovered." Within twenty-four hours, all twelve had left the country.

Guilt can be a powerful force in our lives—for harm and for good. False guilt is not from God, but from the devil, the world, and your own heart. It will only lead you to sorrow, fear, and despair without a desire to restore your fellowship with God. And while genuine guilt will also cause you to feel sorrow, according to II Corinthians 7:9-11, it is the kind of sorrow that leads to repentance and a desire to be cleansed by God.

As followers of Christ, dealing with guilt and experiencing forgiveness from God is a critical aspect of our walk with Him. And before we go any further, it is important that we define what we mean by "forgiveness" here.

There are two kinds of forgiveness you experience as a believer.

• *Judicial forgiveness*—This refers to God's once-and-for-all forgiveness of your sins—past, present, and future (Colossians 1:13, 14; 2:13, 14). It deals with your overall *relationship* to God and your positional standing before Him. This forgiveness occurred when you became a Christian.

• *Parental forgiveness*—This has to do with daily forgiveness in order to restore broken *fellowship* between you and God (Matthew 6:12; I John 1:9). It's like a parent forgiving his or her child. Your intimacy with God is interrupted until your acknowledgment of wrong. This kind of forgiveness cleanses you from daily sin and enables you and the Lord to communicate and enjoy one another's company again. You can experience this forgiveness whenever you sin.

How does a Christian keep his or her fellowship with God fresh and current? How do you bounce back from sin?

Here are three key thoughts to follow when you realize you have sinned:

Step One: Confess it as sin.

I John 1:9
If we confess our sins, he is faithful and just and will forgive us our sins
and purify us from all unrighteousness.

1. What does the phrase "confess your sins" mean?

2. How does that differ from merely admitting that you made a mistake?

Step Two: Consider it forgiven.

3. What does God promise to do for you when you confess your sin?

4. How does Isaiah 1:18 picture this forgiveness?

God will never remember a sin once it is confessed (see Psalm 103:12; Micah 7:19; Isaiah 38:17). It's like the farmer who described forgiveness as "God's throwing our sins into the sea of forgetfulness, and then putting up a sign that says 'No Fishing.'"

Step Three: Continue with life.

5. What if you still feel sinful and guilty, even after you've confessed your sin?

Let's answer that question this way: Suppose you were traveling in another state and got lost in a downtown area. By a minor miracle you see an old friend walking down the street. You ask him for directions to the place you're looking for, and he tells you it's just down the road about a mile. He gives you simple directions and you find it easily.

Once you receive those directions, what is your responsibility?

You could choose to ignore the directions. Or you might think your old friend is lying to you. But more than likely, you would take him at his word and believe them to be the truth.

Now back to our question: What if you still feel sinful and guilty, even after you've confessed your sin? What should you do with God's Word?

Hey, if Jesus isn't going to dwell on your sin and failure any longer, why should you? Trust in God's promise to forgive you and to restore your fellowship and intimacy with Him. In this way, you can keep your walk with God fresh moment by moment.

3 God of the Second Chance

We've already looked at the cleansing and forgiveness that takes place when we confess our sins to the Lord. But there are additional benefits that ought to motivate us to keep short accounts with God and to quickly get back into fellowship with Him.

Look up Psalm 51 in your Bible. David wrote this psalm after he had committed adultery with Bathsheba. (You can read about that in II Samuel 11.)

1. According to Psalm 51:12, what did David know that forgiveness would give him?

2. What other area of his walk with God would be restored? (See verse 13.)

3. What would David be able to do again with a pure heart? (See verses 14 and 15.)

Joy, service, and praise are pretty significant areas of our Christian lives. And they are all damaged when we are in sin. But when we sincerely confess our sins to God, they can be restored to us in full measure. David committed adultery and murder, but God evaluated him in summary to be a man after His own heart (I Samuel 13:14). The Lord obviously didn't say that about David because he never fell into sin. But rather David earned that title because when he did sin, he confessed it and moved on with his life. You can do the same.

On New Year's Day, 1929, Georgia Tech played UCLA in the Rose Bowl. In that game a young player named Roy Riegals recovered a fumble for UCLA. But in picking up the loose ball, he lost his direction and ran at full speed 65 yards in the wrong direction! One of his teammates, Benny Lom, was able to run him down and tackle him just before Roy scored for Georgia Tech. A few plays later, Georgia Tech blocked a UCLA punt and scored on a safety.

At halftime in the locker room, Riegals covered himself in a blanket and sat dejected in a corner alone. Usually the coach had a big speech prepared for halftime, but he was silent that day. When the timekeeper reported that they had three minutes left before playing time, Coach Price looked at his team and said, "Men, the same team that started the first half will start the second half." The players all got up and left—all but Riegals. Coach Price went over to where Riegals was and said, "Roy, didn't you hear me? I want you to start the second half."

Roy Riegals looked up at his coach, his cheeks wet with tears, and said, "Coach, I can't do it. I've ruined you. I've ruined the school's reputation. I've ruined myself. I can't face that crowd out there." Coach Price reached out, put his hand on Roy's shoulder, and said, "Roy, get up and go on back. The game is only half over." Riegals did get up and returned to play an outstanding game.

KEEP In Mind

We've all run in the wrong direction before, perhaps for a long way. But because of the forgiveness we can have through Christ, the game is never over. Failure is never final with Jesus. Failure is just the opportunity to begin once again—this time with a fresh start and more wisdom.

Don't spend your life analyzing every failure. There is no sin too great, no failure too big for God to forgive. Get up. Get forgiven. Get back into fellowship. Get back into the game and play to win!

PRAY About It

Praise God in prayer for His parental forgiveness that cleanses you completely and restores you to your intimacy with Him.

WEEK 15 Graduation Day!

Your Final Glorification in Christ

My Identity: I will stand before Christ in glory one day.

1 It Just Doesn't Get Any Better

Isn't it great to finish something you've started? If you're a runner, it's the race. If you're a student, it's the course. If you're an athlete, it's the game. If you're a reader, it's the book! The feeling of accomplishment, of having done something worthwhile, of completing what you began, is seldom equalled. We've all seen marathon runners fall into the arms of a friend at the finish line, exhausted yet satisfied at the accomplishment. But put all of these together, and they don't come close to equalling the satisfaction that you will know one day when you finish this life and step into the next. It's called being "glorified" in the Bible, and it's the final and most fulfilling step in the journey of your salvation.

Have you ever wondered what it will be like when you get to heaven? Or more importantly, what will *you* be like? How will you be different there? How will your relationship with God be different? What will be waiting there for you? What will it mean to be "glorified"? Why should that excite you now? And how does knowing all of this make a difference in the way you live now? You'll find the answers to these and other questions in this chapter.

2 But He Sure Looked Good

On November 24, 1971, hijacker D. B. Cooper dressed himself in new loafers and an expensive business suit before boarding a Northwest Airlines 727. After takeoff, he promptly demanded two hundred thousand dollars and two sets of parachutes, then bailed out over a densely wooded area of Washington State. Authorities concluded that Cooper's parachutes didn't open, for he was never heard from again.

That's not my idea of "going out in style." However, the Bible does state that Christians will one day exit this world, either through death or Christ's coming, to be transported into the presence of God in heaven. And we won't be wearing an old T-shirt there, either. We'll be clothed with "fine linen, bright and clean" (Revelation 19:8). That's part of what it will mean for us to be "glorified." Now *that's* going out in style!

1. In what ways do the following verses encourage you in this final facet of salvation?

   • II Corinthians 1:21, 22

   • Philippians 1:6

2. What will happen to a Christian's body? (See I Corinthians 15:50-53 and Philippians 3:20, 21.)

These bodies will be awesome, enabling us to do supernatural things (see Luke 24:36-39 and Mark 16:14). At last, you'll have a "heavenly body"!

3. What do you see in Romans 8:30 that tells you about a Christian's future glorification?

3 How Do You Spell Relief?

What will it mean for us to be glorified in heaven? We've already seen that it is promised by God, that it is guaranteed by His Spirit in us, and that it involves having new bodies for believers. But what else will being glorified mean for you?

Here are four words that help describe what it will be like to be glorified in heaven.

Rest

1. We rest when we're tired from something. What do we get tired from in this life that heaven will give us rest from?

- Romans 7:15, 18, 19, 24

- Revelation 21:4

- I Corinthians 15:54-57

Wait a minute! No more temptation or sin? No more pain or sorrow? No more sickness or death? Would you mind taking an eternal rest from these things? Hold on, there's more . . .

Reunion

2. According to I Thessalonians 4:13-17, who will be reunited in glory?

3. Do you have anyone that you're looking forward to seeing? If so, who?

Reward

In glory, God will hold His own "awards ceremony," in which He will reward you for everything you did for Him while on earth. You will receive crowns and an inheritance that will never fade away (I Corinthians 3:11-15; II Corinthians 5:10; I Peter 1:3-5). But the greatest reward of all will be to have God's approval as He says, "Well done, good and faithful servant!" (Matthew 25:21)

Realization

4. What will being glorified change about . . .

• our character or behavior? (See I John 3:2; I Corinthians 1:8; Colossians 1:22; and I Thessalonians 3:13.)

• our sight? (See I John 3:2b.)

• our knowledge? (See I Corinthians 13:9-12.)

4 Heaven in the Real World

You may be asking, "So how should my future glorification in heaven affect my present life here and now?"

It can have a profound affect on four key relationships in your life.

• *Your relationship with Jesus*

1. What does Jesus say is the real meaning of eternal life in John 17:3?

• *Your relationship with other Christians*

2. How does knowing these things affect our relationship with fellow believers? (See I Thessalonians 4:18.)

• *Your relationship to suffering*

3. Looking at Romans 8:18, what perspective does the knowledge of your glorification give to your suffering? (See also II Corinthians 4:17.)

• *Your relationship with yourself*

4. Read I John 3:3. How does the hope of being glorified affect your lifestyle?

Graduation ceremonies are great. Caps and gowns, nervous speeches, friends, and family are all a part of graduations. It's a chance to publicly celebrate the completion of your academic career. Finally, the time comes when your name is called and you walk across that stage. Everyone knows the moment belongs to you. At last, you hold the diploma in your hand.

Maybe you're looking forward to graduating from high school or college. You can't wait to get your diploma and enjoy your academic accomplishment. At times you've wondered if all the hours spent studying are really worth it. You question whether the piece of paper you will receive will make up for all you've had to endure. You try to picture what it will be like to call yourself a "graduate." But nothing you study can fully prepare you for the satisfaction of opening that diploma and seeing your name written so majestically in script. Nothing can help you anticipate the joy of throwing your cap high in the air in celebration. And no person can teach you how to say goodbye to your best friends.

I always look forward to ceremonies like that. And I look back on my own graduations from high school, college, and seminary with great fondness. But there's one more graduation ceremony left for me—and for you. And it's the most important one of all. At this graduation you'll receive much more than a piece of paper. You'll be given eternal rewards and a rich inheritance. And there won't be any more goodbyes, either; only reunions and forever friends then. But the best thing about Graduation Day is at last being embraced by the One whose grace kept you going every step of the way. And that makes everything you do down here worth it all! So keep pressing on for the prize!

KEEP In Mind

Your graduation day is coming. If you're a Christian, you have a Savior and God who love you very much. You've been recreated in Christ and given a new identity. Aren't you blown away now that you realize who you really are in Christ? He has done all that is divinely possible so that you can be with Him forever. Could God be that good?

Count on it!

PRAY About It

Spend this time reviewing in prayer all of the incredible things God has done for you through Christ. Perhaps you could pray a prayer like the one below.

Lord, I am so grateful to You that

You lovingly created and crafted me in Your own image.
I was lost and You found me:
in sin and You made me righteous;
an enemy of God and You made me Your friend;
enslaved to sin and You set me free;
dead and You gave me life;
an orphan and You adopted me;
far away from You and You brought me close;
alone and You gave me a family;
afraid and You calmed my fears.

Therefore, because of Your mercy and grace toward me, I will
seek to grow to maturity,
not abuse my new freedom,
strive to be like Your Son in all things,
keep short accounts with You, and
anxiously await the day when You will complete my salvation.